FIVE MINUTE PHOBIA CURE

Dr. Callahan's Treatment for Fears, Phobias And Self-Sabotage

Roger J. Callahan, Ph.D.

Published by: Enterprise Publishing, Inc.
            725 Market Street
            Wilmington, DE 19801

To My Son, Scott Roger Callahan

Publisher's Note

Even though many people have been helped to date by Dr. Callahan's techniques, there is no guarantee intended or implied that the treatment described in this book will be effective in any specific instance.

In close to a thousand phobias treated, the author has found no evidence that it is harmful to anyone. However, as with all new therapies, you must proceed at your own risk.

If you are in doubt about applicability, you may want to discuss it first with a psychotherapist, doctor or religious counsel.

In some instances what seems to be a phobia may actually be a problem requiring long-term psychological counseling, or the phobia may actually be covering other psychological problems. In such instances it is suggested that a qualified counselor be sought.

If you are taking medication for anxiety, we advise you to consult with a physician before you stop taking the medication or decrease the dosage.

The author and the publisher assume no responsibility, whatsoever, for guaranteeing that any phobia will be effectively treated.

Acknowledgments

No treatment springs full-blown into existence. There must be a gradual merging of concepts — an opening up of new vistas — that permits the doctor to make the quantum leaps that merge them into one new procedure. The "Five-Minute" treatment for phobias is the result of such mergings and conceptualizations.

I want to thank the unknown intellectual giant of China who discovered the human energy system about 5000 years ago, which is just beginning to be explored by Western Science.

Harvey Ross, M.D., deserves my thanks because it was he who first spoke to me of the phenomenon of kinesiologic testing. George Goodheart, D.C., the discoverer of Applied Kinesiology, who uses it in the treatment of physical problems and also is the first chiropractor on the Olympic Medical Team, is also greatly thanked. It was by studying his methods of treatment that I was able to adapt it to work in the healing of psychological problems and phobias.

I acquired much helpful information while attending the 100-hour course in Applied Kinesiology, taught by David S. Walther, D.C., and Robert Blaich, D.C. I wish to thank them for being such superb teachers.

I would also like to thank Iris Bancroft for helping me to express my ideas more clearly, and the wonderful allineated people at Enterprise Publishing, especially my editor Ann Faccenda for her lovely, positive support and considerable help in bringing this work to fruition at last.

Last of all I wish to thank my many patients, without whom I would have learned nothing, and with whom I have been able to experience the exciting joy of quickly and efficiently helping them eliminate their phobias.

Table of Contents

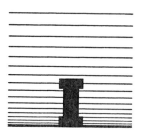

Introduction:

Those Who Are Afflicted

Many people in our society must face life with certain unremediable handicaps. People are born with incomplete bodies, or they lose a limb or sight or hearing because of some accident or illness. But such physical handicaps do not always destroy those individuals who are afflicted. Paraplegics have married, sired or borne children, built careers — and lived happy, fulfilled lives. Blind men and women have learned to enjoy life without vision. All demonstrate the strength of the human spirit. These people daily prove that such handicaps are certainly problems, but they are not absolute destroyers of happiness and fulfillment.

But one handicap does exist that can restrict living until it is almost unbearable. There is one affliction that has the power to destroy all happiness, to limit self-expression, even to lead an individual to seek escape through suicide. This is a common handicap, shared by a higher percentage of people in our society.

This terrible handicap is irrational fear.

People who are possessed by such irrational fears fight a

daily battle for survival. Such chronic fear can ruin careers, destroy human relationships, and deny its victims any happiness or zest for living. Often attempts to overcome the fear by direct assault result not in triumph, but in a strengthening of that fear's hold — as if, like the energy draining invader in Star Trek, fear thrives on its victim's frantic struggle to escape.

I have always had a strong sympathy for persons afflicted with such fears. Irrational fears are burdens that can destroy life itself. I know. I was a phobic child, controlled by useless fears that kept me from enjoying life. My first eleven years were spent in foster homes, and I kept my numerous phobias to myself, suffering in silence. I was frightened of moving —and I had to move often. I feared heights. When I reached college, I was paralyzed when asked to speak before my class. I dreaded entering a tunnel — any tunnel, no matter how short. I feared new places. I was afraid to look up at the night sky, for fear I would see "destruction raining down upon me."

Most of my fears had no basis in reality. But this did not make them any less real. Suffice it to say that I developed a general anxiety pattern in my approach to life, while at the same time "adjusting" so as to live with my fears. It was not a happy solution, but it is one that is still used by many phobics. Adjust, allow for the limitations the phobia imposes, and try to go on with life.

I certainly followed an expected pattern. I took up psychology because I was "interested" in the subject. It is possible that I also had an underlying desire to cure myself —and to better understand my childhood affliction.

Considering my personal experience, it is not surprising that my doctoral dissertation was on the subject of children's fears. I also developed a psychological test to measure levels of anxiety in an attempt to better understand the problem.

When I began a private practice, many of my patients

sought help in overcoming phobias. Perhaps they sensed my empathy and kinship with them. I'm sure that even though many had few expectations of every being fully cured, they knew that they would at least be treated with understanding.

My first book, **It Can Happen to You: The Practical Guide to Romantic Love,** had as its theme the concept of amorophobia (a term I coined), which I defined as the fear, usually subconscious, of being psychologically devastated by romantic rejection. In that book, as in my general practice, I was concerned with the fears men and women have that destroy happiness. I wanted to help these lonely people who let fear keep them from self-realization.

Like my associates, I did the best I could for sufferers who came to me, using a combination of some of the therapies listed in Chapter 2, but I knew all along that I was asking a patient to endure pain every time I asked him to confront his fear. And so, I continued to read and investigate, hoping to find a more efficient approach — a way that would minimize pain and the need for such agonizing confrontations with the cause of the terror. I wanted more than to *diminish* my patients' phobias — I wanted to *cure* them.

My search led, finally, to the treatment discussed in this book.

I have now used my treatment on my patients, freeing them from hundreds of phobias — and the results have been dramatic. I have treated subjects who feared heights, flying, snakes, spiders, people who feared social contacts, talking on the telephone, riding horses, singing before an audience, parties, impotence, and even computers. In 85 percent of the cases, I have been able to effect almost instantaneous, pain-less, natural cures.

It certainly appears that the cure is lasting. Years have passed since I treated my first patients in this new manner, and those with whom I am still in contact have shown no recurrence of the phobias.

Throughout my life, I have been personally and professionally involved with fears and phobias. I know how destructive they can be. So I feel fortunate that I have had the opportunity to participate in the development of this pain-free, natural treatment. To the best of my knowledge, there has never been any treatment for a psychological problem that has approached the power, effectiveness, efficiency and permanence of the techniques described in the following pages.

(Note: A phobia is a persistent, irrational fear which usually causes significant discomfort. The terms *fear* and *phobia* are used interchangeably in this book, unless otherwise specified.)

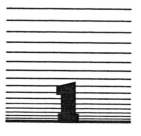

The
Fear
Factor

Useful Fear

Throughout the history of mankind, fear has served a useful purpose. The primitive hunter knew fear when he tracked the mammoth beasts that roamed wild around him, and that fear made him cautious — thereby extending his life. The tightrope walker knows fear that keeps him alert and channels his concentrations on the rope which he must traverse. We are taught to be cautious when we cross streets, climb rocks, walk in the desert, so that we will not be hit by cars, fall from a great height or tread on a rattler. We can all describe fears that benefit us — that extend our lives and keep us safe from obvious danger.

So it is clear to us all that fear *can* be a very beneficial emotion. It causes an individual to exert caution in a hazardous situation. It protects an individual from unnecessary risk taking. When it plays this role in life, fear sharpens the senses and makes a person more alert to indications of danger.

All of us have, at one time or another, felt such useful fear. We must walk through a dangerous section of town, and we feel our adrenaline supply increase. We have a heightened sense of hearing — an awareness of movements around us that we would miss were we walking down a lighted street in a "good" part of town. So we stay clear of empty store fronts and dark passages. We complete our errands and hurry on our way to safer environs.

Or we decide to go swimming in the ocean. "Useful" fear inspires caution. We do not swim out as far as we can, taxing our strength so that we cannot make it back to shore.

Fear guides our judgment in such situations — valuable fear. Even though we feel apprehension when we are influenced by that fear, it does not cripple our minds or keep us from actions that would make life more fulfilling. Instead, it keeps us safe from death and injury — both laudable goals.

An excellent example of such valuable fear is found during a battle. We often hear of the "fearlessness" of soldiers. But the fact is that a good soldier is not fearless. On the contrary, a man who actually feels no fear makes a poor soldier, for he is apt to get himself and his comrades into situations that could end their lives and risk the success of the fight.

Characteristically, fear produces definite, recognizable physical and psychological reactions. At the onset of fear, adrenaline is pumped into the bloodstream, muscles grow tense, the palms become sweaty, breathing becomes rapid, and the heartbeat increases. The body is preparing to respond to an emergency. We still experience the "fight or flight" response that saved the lives of primitive men. In this form, and when situations warrant the need for life-saving action, fear is appropriate.

Degrees of Fear

Because fears come in different degrees and contexts, we have different words to describe them. If you are *worried* because you or a loved one must drive through the mountains in a heavy snowstorm, the worry fits the situation. The emotion may cause a muscle tenseness and a slight increase in heartbeat, but normally none of the symptoms will be so severe as to keep you from carrying on normal functions. The worry fades away when the ride is over, and so do the symptoms.

Other words denote other levels of fear. We have all felt *nervous* at one time or another. But some individuals are *terrified* in a situation that in most people will arouse nervousness.

Almost everyone has at one time or another felt *anxious* about the results of a medical examination.

If any of these fears are experienced moderately and vanish when the circumstances which occasioned them are gone, we generally acknowledge that it was "foolish to worry," or "not sensible to feel anxious." Even an individual who is anxious while awaiting the results of a physical examination will admit that his anxiety contributed nothing to the prognosis.

What makes many of these fears acceptable is the degree to which we feel them. They exist in response to some circumstance, and fade away when the situation changes. Even though they are often useless, they do not cause us any great concern.

Useful and Useless Fears

The student who is worried about passing an examination determines by his actions the category of his fear. If it spurs him to study, to systematically apply his mind to mastering those subjects in which he is weak, then his worry is useful. Because of it, he improves his knowledge and passes his examination.

If he frets about the questions he believes he will answer wrong, retreats into a "bad mood," and refuses to do anything that might improve his chances of passing, then his worry is useless. More than that — it is destructive.

If fears such as *anxiety, embarrassment, nervousness,* and *worry* do not motivate us to act to improve our situation, they are useless fears. Fears are useless, if they are out of proportion to the situation that causes them to develop. Thus a high school student who fears he may fail one test and therefore ruin his entire life is experiencing an unrealistic fear. One high school test is not that crucial. Similarly, the man who fears a mouse and cannot even approach it or look at it is experiencing an unreasonable fear. Mice do not pose a threat to human life.

But were the student to face the possibility that he might fail to graduate from high school and not qualify for college, he would be confronting a situation that *could* "ruin" his life, and were a man to fear a rattler and avoid it as he walks, his fear would be useful. A rattler *could* bite him and cause him physical harm.

Like all human emotions, useless fears must be seen in perspective. If the level of a useless fear is low and it does not interfere with normal living, the person experiencing it may forget it as soon as the stimulus that brought it to his attention is eliminated. But if the fear does not go away, it may "linger on," controlling and influencing his life. Such long-lasting fears, even "small" ones, can have far-reaching influence on a person who experiences them. He feels less than adequate when he knows he suffers from irrational fears. So, for many reasons, they should be eliminated.

Hidden Fears

One of the characteristics of fear is that it does not always show itself for what it is. Fears can be hidden as a protective measure. The mind cannot face the fear directly, and so it builds defenses, creates a character, that will save the person from experiencing that fear.

A shy individual may appear to be simply a "private person," but may in fact be terrified of meeting new people. Lack of recognition of his deep fear keeps him from the pleasure of being with others.

A compulsive person who insists on perfection in everything he does may actually be suffering from hidden fear. Yet all the observer sees is that this person "makes much over" errors or mistakes that other people seem able to accept.

Acute sensitivity, shyness, timidity, over-aggressiveness, volatile temperament, fetishistic sex behavior, depression, all can conceal fears of which the victim is not aware. These behavior patterns cause individuals to make life-affecting decisions. The sensitive or the timid individual may avoid certain jobs where he might have his feelings easily hurt. He may stay in a menial task because he can't "stand up" and assume a role of authority.

An over-aggressive person, or an individual who is easily angered, may offend superiors by his actions, and thus lose opportunities for promotions. Yet, if he were to "fix blame" for his lack of advancement, he would not consider that fear might be the true cause.

A man who fears talking to women may be able to avoid such situations most of the time, but his shyness might keep him from meeting a woman with whom he could have a fulfilling, romantic relationship. Similarly, a woman who feared closeness might, whenever she felt an emotional closeness developing, create problems that resulted in upsets and an eventual break-up. Yet neither one of them would be apt to blame fear for their lack of happiness.

Many people display obsessive behavior, constant headaches, compulsive cleanliness, sleeplessness, sexual problems, asthma, stuttering, depression, timidity, over aggressiveness, or uncertainty about their role in the world. Often, these reactions dominate a person's life, and yet he will not realize that fear has anything to do with it.

The tragedy is that such sufferers usually do not believe they have a disability serious enough to require therapy. They learn to live with a life-diminishing affliction, and often the behavior it engenders becomes habitual. They cease to consider that they have a problem at all.

Phobias

Like minor "useless" fears, phobias serve no purpose —they are irrational — out of proportion to the situations that call them up. A phobia is a persistent disproportionate or inappropriate fear. The phobic *knows* that his fear is inappropriate, but his knowledge does not help him overcome it. In fact, this awareness usually complicates things by adding shame and embarrassment to the phobia. The basic feature of phobia is that the fear is unrealistic or disproportionate to the situation.

Phobias, like "normal fear reactions," cause an increase in heartbeat. They may bring about a rise in blood pressure, a tension in the muscles, quickness of breath, and sweaty palms. Unlike "useful" fears, they overwhelm an individual, restricting his ability to act. They are out of proportion to the situation that seems to trigger them. And often, they appear to be brought on spontaneously.

A woman who spends thirty years in her apartment, irrationally fearful of stepping outside, even for a moment, is a victim of such fear. In a very real way, fear destroys her life. Yet such an extreme case is not unusual.

Robert L. DuPont, director of Washington's Center for Behavior Medicine, calls phobias "the malignant disease of the 'what-if's." A more popular description is that phobias are "the exponential growth of imaginary disasters that can choke off rational thought." These irrational fears are so powerful that they motivate individuals to make life-altering decisions that are not in their best interests. Phobics know only too well the negative strength of their affliction.

The insidious thing about such an irrational fear (inappropriate to the cause) is that it can be triggered by any object, thought, person, memory, situation, creature, concept, or emotional state. One can be irrationally afraid of emotional closeness, of touching, or "opening up" to someone else. One can fear horses, mice, cats, kittens, trees, space, malls, dentists, shopping, speaking in public. There seems to be no area of human experience, nor any object in existence that cannot become the object of irrational fear. And once this inappropriate fear is established, it usually grows in strength.

It seems unnecessary to itemize the many kinds of phobias with which humans can be tormented. Yet a few will indicate the scope of the problem. Individuals have suffered from *Acrophobia* (fear of heights), *Aerophobia* (fear of flying), *Anthophobia* (fear of flowers), *Claustrophobia* (fear of closed spaces), *Numerophobia* (fear of numbers), *Gephyrophobia* (fear of bridges), *Agorophobia* (fear of open places), and *Xenophobia* (fear of strangers). But naming fears in this manner contributes little to this cure. An individual's fear of dogs is no less real because he calls it *Cynophobia.*

These phobias can be directed into every aspect of human existence. One person may fear tight places. Another may dread the sight of a newspaper or the sound of running water. No area of human experience is safe from the ravages of phobia. Blood, even one drop of it, may put a phobic individual into a state of panic. But so can a certain sound, an odor, a memory, or an act performed by another person.

One out of every nine adults harbors some kind of phobia. The percentage would be even greater were we to include mild phobias, disguised fears, and compulsive behavior that is rooted in fear. Phobias compose the nation's most common mental health problem. There is even some evidence that many people are alcoholics because of a need to hide from the terror of unacknowledged phobias.

Is it enough to describe phobias as "irrational fears"? How do they start? Are they always rooted in some frightening past experience? I do not believe that they are.

Phobias are usually spontaneous in nature, and they may attach themselves to specific objects or situations. Patients today seek help in overcoming fear of flying, of having space debris fall on their heads, of computers and automatic typewriters. Those specific fears could not have existed before the objects or modes of travel existed. So it appears that there will be no shortage of situations and objects that can be the subject of phobias, even if mankind reaches the far edges of the solar system.

Can Phobias be Learned?

We deliberately teach our children some fears — and rightly so. Children must learn that running into the street is dangerous. They must be taught to stay away from strangers, especially men who might try to lure them into a car or away from adult protection. They must learn to respect electricity, boiling water, fire, poisonous substances, moving automobiles. But this "fear for safety" instruction does not result in phobias. I have treated people who had a phobic reaction to sunflowers and trees, but I have never encountered anyone, no matter how strictly trained to avoid electric outlets, who exhibited a phobic reaction to such objects.

Many times, phobias seem to "just happen." A person can go for years with no reaction to traveling through a tunnel and then, unexpectedly, for no apparent reason, face his next such journey in a state of mortal terror.

It would certainly, be wrong to say that phobias *never* are "learned." Every psychologist has encountered a phobic whose condition is a direct result of some trauma. We meet the boy who fears all dogs because he was bitten when a child, the woman who fears falling because, as a young girl, she slipped while climbing a hill and was saved from death only because she landed in a bramble bush that broke her fall —the adult who fears water because, as an infant, he was exposed to a terrible storm that frightened him. But such cares are not as common as is often supposed. Most phobias are not rooted in experience.

Theories Regarding the Development of Phobias

For years sufferers have been told that their phobias had psychological bases. Freud, the first to present that concept, took careful notes during therapy sessions and was convinced that the terrors and panics that afflicted his patients had their roots in childhood conflicts. It was, he decided, easier for a son to develop a phobia than to face the jealously and anger he felt toward his father. And Freud was convinced that such feelings of jealously and anger were common in children.

In 1966, Dr. Ferris Pitts, professor of psychiatry at the University of Southern California, showed that injections of sodium lactate can trigger panic attacks, but only in people who also have such attacks spontaneously. Antidepressant drugs may also have the same effect on individuals who have spontaneous attacks. This indicated that phobias might have a physical origin.

Dr. Donald F. Klein, director of psychiatric research at the New York State Psychiatric Institute, found that one anti-depressant drug, *Imipramine,* served to lessen panic attacks in his patients. He concluded that at least some phobic attacks might resemble a "physiological discontinuity, as with pneumonia and colds." Thus, an antidepressant drug might have no effect on a *mild* phobic reaction (as penicillin has very little effect on a cold), but it might work against a *strong* panic attack (as penicillin can and does cure pneumonia). This served to reinforce the concept that phobias were caused by abnormal physical conditions.

There is evidence that some types of individuals are predisposed to phobias, just as some people are especially susceptible to tuberculosis or cancer — or heart attacks or strokes. Dr. David V. Sheehan, director of anxiety research at the Massachusetts General Hospital in Boston and author of *The Anxiety Disease,* has added his voice to those who believe that panic attacks are not psychological in origin at all. Dr. Sheehan has stated that phobias are "a real disease, resulting from a genetic vulnerability."

There is increasing evidence that a correlation exists between certain physical ailments and a tendency toward phobias. Dr. Harvey Ross, a psychiatric authority on hypoglycemia, reports that many of his phobic patients are also hypoglycemic.

These new discoveries often combine with the many other theories in existence and totally confuse the layman who seeks some knowledge of the problem. It is easy to see why this is so. At present, every theory regarding the cause of phobias seems to have its contingent of supporters, each group "putting down" the claims of the others. What is important to remember is that the test of the theory lies in the cure.

Psychological theorists are sometimes brilliantly creative in providing intricate dynamics which purport to explain the psychological origins of phobias. Although these notions may be very clever, they are, in my opinion, rarely accurate.

There is an interesting similarity between allergies and phobias. Both seem to develop spontaneously. Both have a genetic predisposition to occur. And both are evidenced by a confusion of the responses which should serve to protect the human organism from harm.

The *immune system* exists to automatically counteract any dangerous substance or chemical (germs, viruses, foreign matter) that might enter the parameters of the body. *Allergies* have been found to be the result of the immune system gone haywire. The immune system, somehow no longer able to identify true danger, "defends" the body against a harmless substance.

Like the automatic action of the physical immune system, the *psychological defense system* is designed to protect the body from danger. Phobias seem to be the result of the psychological defense system gone awry. The sweaty palms, palpitations, increased heart-beat, and flow of adrenaline are all symptoms of the "fight or flight" response that, in truly dangerous situations, are lifesaving. But when no real danger exists, these responses can, in themselves, stress the human organism.

I believe that some people are genetically prone to develop phobias and others are prone *not* to develop phobias no matter what happens to them. In all cases of phobia, the bottom line is that there is a disturbance in the body energy distribution system.

In the approach used herein, phobias are seen as a disruption of normal energy flows in the body. These energy flows have been recognized for thousands of years by the Chinese, who utilize them when they treat pains and ills with acupuncture. Dr. Goodheart and other practitioners of applied kinesiology take the presence of these energies into consideration when they use applied kinesiology to treat physical disorders, thereby correcting body dysfunctions and imbalances. (More regarding this will be found in Chapter 3.)

I find the above way of looking at a phobia to be very useful in the "Five-Minute" treatment. The cure serves to open up the blockages that created the phobia, and the phobia is eliminated.

Myths That Surround Phobias

Possibly because phobias are so common and so difficult to eliminate, many myths have grown up to support the idea that phobias have value. Creative people often credit their phobias for their creativity and look down on non-creative individuals who "haven't the imagination" to have phobias.

They seem to have some justification for their conceit. It appears that there *is* some relationship between the ability to imagine graphically and a susceptibility to phobias. Actors, creative writers, artists, seem to have a greater problem with phobias than do persons with less imagination.

Are they right when they claim phobic behavior as indicative of creative talent?

I think not. There is a far greater possibility that these people, depending as they do upon their creativity for their livelihood, are quicker to seek help than are people who, because their work is not affected too badly by a phobia, resign themselves to "living with it." So more creative people acknowledge their phobias, sometimes even feel pride in having them, while persons who are not as creative tend to "cover up" similar conditions.

Yet, it is not only creative people who cling to their phobias. Many people with phobias insist that their fears are beneficial. When the 1971 earthquake occurred in the San Fernando Valley, in California, causing a collapse of an over-pass, a phobic person who feared even short tunnels used that collapse as "proof" that his fear was justified — and lifesaving.

As a result, he became even more convinced that his fear was reasonable, even though it had confined him to living in the valley for many years, and caused him to drive miles out of his way to avoid overpasses.

This tendency of many phobics to cling to their phobias with a determination that seems to indicate that they truly do not wish to lose them serves only to confuse most non-afflicted friends and relatives. Why should a person whose life is limited by fear resist all "logical" explanations that refute the need for fear? Why do the phobic never accept the "proof," offered by non-phobic friends, that his phobia is foolish?

The fact is that a person who has never experienced the terror of phobia cannot understand the dilemma the phobic faces. The phobic recognizes only too well that his fear is unreasonable. He *"knows"* that he is stupid to be so afflicted. He "puts himself down" because of his fear, and his self-denigration seriously compounds his problem.

Kinds of Phobias

It is not uncommon for laypeople to assume that all phobics are alike. For example that they all fear some specific object, situation, or event. The fact is that psychologists classify phobias into two groups: simple phobias and compound phobias.

Simple phobias, because they can be "worked around," often do not interfere with "normal" interaction between the phobic and the subject of his fear. A fear of needles is such a simple fear. So is the fear of cats, dogs, tunnels, escalators, bats — objects which generally can be avoided, thus permitting the subject to bypass his fear. A person who fears airplanes, for example, can simply insist that one "misses so much beautiful scenery" when one flies, and thus pretend, even to himself, that his avoidance of planes has nothing to do with fear. This "avoidance as a solution" is the basic characteristic of simple fears.

Only when a simple fear actually interferes with an individual's living does it have to be faced at all. For example, Aretha Franklin might have been able to pretend that she preferred to drive rather than fly from one concert appearance to the next when she suddenly experienced a spontaneous phobic reaction to flying. But the sudden occurrence of this unexpected fear coincided with a concert tour in which she had scheduled concerts every day. When she found that, after years of flying without fear she just could not board the plane, her phobia had to be acknowledged — and she missed her concert.

Had Ms. Franklin been able to make use of the "Five-Minute" treatment, she would not have had to alter her schedule and disappoint a stadium full of fans. Even though simple phobias may be restrictive, as was Aretha Franklin's phobia, they are generally easy to cure with the "Five-Minute" treatment. And once they are gone, they do not return.

Sometimes, simple phobias are so hidden by rationalization that it is difficult to ferret them out. *Insomnia* presents a good example of this. Some people just can't get to sleep without the use of "sleeping pills." When they come to therapy for help, it may be necessary to discover the underlying fear before the insomnia can be treated. Some real fear may be keeping the victim awake. A fear he dare not face. More on this in a later chapter.

Compound phobias, on the contrary, limit an individual's ability to be around other people and to interact with them. *Amorophobia,* the fear of falling in love, is a compound phobia because it severely handicaps its victim. An Amorophobic cannot experience intense romantic relationships. He or she panic when another person begins to "get too close."

Compound phobias are composed of many fears. *Amorophobia,* for example, may include fear of rejection, fear of being ugly, fear of being offensive, fear of sexual embarrassment, even fear of being accepted sexually. It may include fear of exposing some deep private secret. These involvements make curing compound phobias far more difficult than curing simple phobias. More will be said regarding this problem in a later chapter.

An *agoraphobic* may be so frightened of leaving home that she will literally imprison herself within her room. *Agoraphobia* literally means fears of the marketplace. Today, the name is applied to a general fear of many connecting circumstances. An agoraphobic will usually fear many things and/or situations, such as open spaces, crowds, the feeling that things are happening behind her, the expanse of the sky — many fears which she usually doesn't isolate. (I speak of "her" here because, for some unknown reason, most *agoraphobics* are women.)

Agoraphobia may be complicated by hypoglycemia, and some agoraphobics may show symptoms which clinicians would consider schizophrenic, or label borderline psychotic. Such cases are too complicated for a layperson to handle, though it may be possible to use the "Five-Minute" treatment with enough success to at least get the patient out of the house and into a therapist's office.

For most phobics, however, such complications do not exist. An individual may be very "normal" in every way except for his unreasoning fear of heights, or closed spaces, or snakes, or some other object or situation. These people, for whom a phobia is a life-limiting problem that is not connected in some way to another physical ailment, have sought help from psychologists and psychotherapists, since no medical problems complicate the cure. These sufferers from "simple" phobias have — and still do — account for a great number of the patients who currently seek psychotherapy.

Throughout the generations, psychotherapists have struggled to cure these sufferers. Their goals have always been the same — to relieve pain — but their methods of cure, dependent as they were on the reigning theories concerning the cause of phobias were not always as successful as one would wish them to be.

Phobia Treatments
An Investment
In Time and Pain

Just as the attempt to establish the origin and the cause of phobias has continued through the years, so also has the search for the perfect cure. Today, a person with behavior problems that mask an inner face, or a man or woman who is phobic, has many options when it comes to seeking help. True, these options have changed over the years. But it would be wrong to assume that because treatment seems to be changing all the time, it is not effective.

The "improvements" in treatment come from the therapist's desire to lighten the burden his patient carries — to simplify and speed up the cure. This casts no aspersions on what was done in the past; understanding of causes of phobias and fears was more restricted then. But as we gain more knowledge of what causes phobias, we can improve our methodology — and cure more patients more efficiently. It is valuable, therefore, to understand past treatments, and to see how I was lead to the discovery of the "Five-Minute" treatment.

Students of Freud developed and elaborated on this theory that a phobia was a "protective" mental affliction that kept its victim from facing the far more painful knowledge that he feared that his father would castrate him. They spent endless hours with their patients, searching through childhood memories in hopes of relocating that critical moment when a specific fear first developed. The tragedy is that far too often that long-anticipated discovery, when finally achieved, did nothing to alleviate the phobia. More to the point is the fact that many phobics are intimately aware of the conditions which surrounded their first phobic attack, yet this knowledge does nothing to alleviate the condition.

So traditional Freudian psychology is not generally practiced today. Modern therapists recognize that the old theory that all phobias and fears have roots in childhood resentment of parents does not hold water. As the theories regarding the *cause* of phobias changed, so did the cures. All of them, to one degree or another, have been rewarded with success.

The problem is that though therapists might have advocated some specific cure, patients often could face the long years of treatment and the painful confrontations that were involved. And therein lay the problem. Each treatment had its price — in money and pain. A number of the most accepted "cures" are *Flooding, Conditioned Reflex, Behavioral Therapy, Neurolinguistic Training, Clinical Hypnosis,* and *Rational Emotive Therapy.* Each is introduced and explained below.

Flooding

One accepted treatment, and the one that probably is at

the top of the chart as being the most painful, is *flooding*. This method was first reported in 1938, when a young doctor, whose name is lost in history, possibly impulsively attempting to use a "sink or swim" method of fighting his young female patient's fear of cars, ordered her to be driven from her home to his office in Manhattan. The trip involved a drive of about an hour and a half, and included traversing the Holland Tunnel as well as crossing several bridges, all of which the doctor knew made his patient especially anxious.

She was in a state of panic on the day of her visit, suffering from nausea and faintness. Her anxiety continued for most of the drive, but as she approached her doctor's office, it subsided. To her delight, her anxiety was not as strong on the return journey, and it gradually diminished with each subsequent trip.

The first technical description of flooding was written by Dr. Nicholas Malleson, in his book *Panic and Phobia,* published in 1959. He utilized the method to treat a young Indian student who was in panic because he feared he might fail his exams and bring shame on his family back in India. Dr. Malleson had his patient imagine the worst shame that he might face were he to return home a failure, including his mother's tears, the scorn directed in his direction by his peers, his wife's devastation and unhappiness.

At first, when he followed the directions of Dr. Malleson, the young man's distress increased. But with each reception of the fantasy, the reaction grew weaker. It became more and more difficult for the youth to maintain vivid images of his shame. And as the visualization grew weaker, so did his reactions. Within a half an hour he was calm. The treatment was repeated twice a day during the two days that preceeded his examinations, and by the time he sat for the tests, he was almost totally unable to feel fright. He passed with no difficulty.

In modern flooding, the therapist arranges to expose his patient to relatively strong "doses" of whatever it is he fears. The presentation lasts until the fear symptoms begin to fade, which normally take somewhere between ten minutes and an hour. Each session sees a further diminution of the phobic reactions. If flooding is successful, the patient finally reaches a point where he can face the object of his phobia without terror. The fear is conquered. The anxiety habit is weakened to where it no longer has power to control.

It is not understood exactly how flooding works. What is assumed is that the individual experiences what Pavlov called protective inhibition. This is a response similar to that which develops when an individual is exposed to a loud noise. At first the noise is insufferable, causing extreme distress. But soon the response to the noise diminishes until it reaches endurable proportions, even though the noise itself has not lessened. This is assumed to be caused by a built-in mechanism in the body that protects it from too much excitation.

There is also one other factor. If the therapist is present during flooding, the treatment has been found to be far more effective than it is when he is absent. Possibly the comfort afforded by the therapist's closeness competes with the fear, serving to diminish it. This might be why the young girl in the above example felt better as she approached her doctor's office.

The major difficulty with flooding is that it is very stressful. Many times the pain occasioned by an episode of flooding is so severe that the patient refuses to continue therapy. Obviously, if treatment is stopped before a cure is completed, the therapy cannot be considered effective.

Conditioned Reflex Therapy

Andrew Salter brought out his edition of *Conditioned Reflex Therapy* in 1949. At the time it was an isolated, bold and heretical statement against the then pervasive and established psychoanalytic approach to the treatment of phobias and fears. Salter was very critical of the philosophy and the inefficiency of psychoanalysis. He based his approach on the more rigorous work of Pavlov (the Russian psychologist who established the concept of the "conditioned reflex").

The Conditioned Reflex approach was a highly directed approach, designed to interfere with the neural patterns formed by neurotic habits. Each time a phobic patient made any progress in overcoming his or her phobia, he or she would be rewarded by the therapist. Salter has a private practice, and he succeeded in curing his patients in a far shorter time than possible through psychoanalysis. Nevertheless, even his treatment took months before a cure was complete.

Behavioral Therapy

Therapy designed to alter a patient's response to a fear-causing situation is *Behavioral Therapy*. Within this blanket exist many different approaches. All have roots in the basic ideas that if a patient is relaxed and enjoying himslf, a feared object may be introduced in a non-threatening manner. Each time this feared object is brought closer, but never so quickly as to arouse fear.

For example, a child who fears rabbits may be given a favorite candy. While he is eating, a toy bunny is brought into the room, but kept as far from the child as possible. The child is made aware of the bunny, but no threat is made to bring the toy close. Each time the child is brought in for treatment, the toy bunny is moved closer. Over a long period of time, the child becomes accustomed to associating the bunny with the pleasure of eating his favorite candy — not with the fear that it had once caused. When the child can play with the toy without fear, a real rabbit is brought in and the process is repeated, if necessary.

Another form of Behavior Therapy utilizes hypnosis. Some therapists hypnotize their patients and then plant suggestions that will "override" the fear brought on by the phobia. They may also use the hypnotic condition to ferret out the cause of some specific phobia.

Behavioral Therapy, especially in the form of relaxation therapy utilizing *systematic desensitization* (where fears are faced in order of severity and overcome while the patient is in a state of relaxation) is in common use today. It is based on a logical, systematic confronting of a series of fears in the following manner:

Together, patient and therapist rank the patient's fears in order of severity. Those which produce the greatest anxiety are put on the top of the list. Those that incur the least anxiety on the bottom. Then, in a very relaxed condition, the patient is asked to picture stressful situations, beginning with those which are lowest in his list. This way, the least fearful situations are the first confronted and overcome. With each session fears higher up the scale are confronted until they have all been laid to rest.

Joseph Wolpe, M.D., author of *Our Useless Fears,* in which he details this technique, indicates that "80 and 90 percent of patients are either apparently cured or much improved after an average of *twenty-five to thirty sessions.*". (Italics are mine.)

Such a claim, backed by the evidence he presents, is impressive. No other treatment dependent upon a series of consecutive sessions with a therapist is more successful.

Nevertheless, there are failures in all of these systems of treatment, failures that are not recognized until the patient has endured many sessions of therapy and much expense. This possibility of failure, coupled with the length of time needed for success, and the recognition of the pain necessary during treatment causes some phobics to refuse to ever begin therapy.

When a fear is so great that even thinking about the feared object overwhelms an individual, he cannot be expected to voluntarily subject himself to months of treatment that depend upon his concentration on that frightening object. And so many phobic go untreated even when their phobia restricts them severely.

Neuro Linguistic Programming

Neuro Linguistic programming was developed by Bandler and Grindler after they studied the procedures of therapists whose work they considered especially effective, especially the work of Milton Erickson, the clinical hypnotist.

Bandler and Grindler concluded that human experience is encoded in an individualized series of representational systems that corresponds to the sensory systems one uses to make contact with the world, principally *visual, auditory,* and *kinesthetic* modalities. They believe that each individual has his own preferred modality, and that if they can contact a phobic person in the modality he "prefers," they will have greater success in curing the phobia, because client-therapist rapport will be increased. They also set as one of their goals that of helping a patient who limits his modality to one area to expand his awareness of his surroundings through the use of the other modalities.

Some doctors are now using this approach in treating phobias. However, some investigative psychologists suggest that neuro linguistics may not be valid as a method of helping people overcome their emotional problems.* Obviously, the final word has not yet been said regarding this procedure.

Clinical Hypnosis

Clinical Hypnosis has been used for many years in both medicine and psychology. The exact nature of the hypnotic state is not yet understood, but it is known that though it appears to be similar to sleep it is not actually sleep. A patient who is hypnotized is aware of his surroundings, can answer questions, and even move about, but if he is told that a certain portion of his body has no feeling, he will believe it and show no indication of pain if that area is hurt. The most dramatic use of hypnosis is to provide anaesthesia for major surgery in subjects who respond to suggestion. For decades it was known that this worked, but only recently research has shown that the procedure releases *endorphins,* the body's natural pain killer.

---

*Gunn, W.B.; Walker, M.K., and Day, H.D.

Different hypnotists utilize different procedures to treat phobias. For example, the subject might be given a positive suggestion while he is hypnotized. A person who fears heights might be told while under hypnosis that he is climbing to a height and that he feels fine, enjoys the scene, and is elated by the altitude. He might then be told that he will awaken, remembering how he felt during his "climb," and that his feeling will persist whenever he climbs or finds himself on a high place.

It is important that the suggestions given be positive. (The patient should be given only positive information regarding altitude.) This works because relaxation (as induced in hypnotism) is antagonistic to the tension induced by fear.

In some patients, this method is effective, lasting for a considerable time. In others, though there may be an immediate improvement, the phobic condition soon returns. Yet others seem unable to respond to this form of therapy and show no improvement, even immediately after treatment. This corresponds to the results reported in the use of hypnotism as a "cure" for smoking or alcoholism.

Rational Emotive Therapy

Dr. Albert Ellis, confronted with the ineffectiveness of conventional Freudian therapy in combating psychological problems, concluded that the problem lay in the patient's inability to deeply recognize, on an emotional level, the illogic of this fear. He devised Rational Emotive Therapy, (R.E.T.) in which the patient "dominates" his fear. This is done through repetitive exposures to the fear-producing situation during which he repeatedly reminds himself that the fear is irrational and challenges the deep-seated convictions that created the problem.

It works. I used R.E.T. to overcome phobias of my own as well as those of numerous patients.

As I mentioned earlier, I feared looking up because I was certain I would see "destruction raining down upon me." Yet I "knew" that the sky did not hold such danger. I overcame my fear by forcing myself to look up, despite my terror, all the while reminding myself, over and over again, that my fear was irrational, that I was creating my own fear by saying sentences to myself such as "how horrible the sky is at night." In time, I "dominated" my fear.

But my cure did not take place swiftly, nor without extreme discomfort. Like flooding, R.E.T. is painful. It takes courage to face fears directly, even fears that one knows are "unrealistic."

Yet, this logical approach to phobias is one of the most successful to date. The cures that are effected by it endure, and the pain experienced often is not as severe as that experienced during flooding. Today, many successful therapists treat their patients using the R.E.T. approach.

The major difficulty with R.E.T. is that many patients are not willing to endure the lengthy months or years of pain and discomfort as they force themselves to confront their fears and phobias. When they are not cured quickly, they discontinue therapy altogether, resorting, instead, to "adjusting" their lives to accommodate their phobias.

The Search For Something Better

During my thirty years of practice as a therapist, I utilized many of these methods of treatment. But always I felt a dissatisfaction, both with the time involved and with the degree of discomfort I inflicted upon my patients. I knew only too well that some patients could not endure, either financially or emotionally, the long periods needed to effect a cure. I realized also, that others seemed to resist cure, even when all the circumstances surrounding the treatment seemed to point to a satisfactory end to their problems.

It was during my search for some quicker, less painful way to a cure my patients that I encountered applied kinesiology. In it, I found the key for which I had been searching. Using it, I was finally able to devise the cure which I now call the "Five-Minute" treatment for phobias.

The Birth
of a
Treatment

I first encountered applied kinesiology when a friend came back from a conference I had been unable to attend and described an arm muscle test that had been used in a seminar. The test is such that it can result in the arm "going weak" if the subject tells an untruth. For example, a man can hold his arm stiff and resist downward pressure if he gives his true name when asked to tell who he is, but if he gives a false name, his arm weakens.

The idea that mental attitude could so directly affect body reactions intrigued me. I investigated further and subsequently attended a course in applied kinesiology, taught by David S. Walther, D.C., and Robert Blaich, D.C. I was the only psychologist present. I was not at all certain that what they had to say could have any application to my practice.

In their course, I learned about body meridians and energy flows, both of which have been used in applied kinesiology to treat sports injuries and other physical ailments. According to applied kinesiology the body is divided into a number of meridians, each including some vital organ as well as considerable skin surface. When a meridian becomes blocked for one reason or another, illness or pain results. Rhythmic tapping at a specific point on a meridian will improve the condition of the associated vital organ. This, they say, occurs because the "energy flow" within that meridian is freed to move again.

Gradually, I began to see connections that permitted me to take what I had learned and adapt it to psychological problems. Through repeated observations, I concluded that phobic reactions were usually connected to a problem in the stomach meridian. One of the "treatment points" for the stomach meridian is the second toe (on both feet). Tapping both toes at the right spot balanced the flow of energy in the stomach meridian.

My first subject for this new treatment was a woman who had lived most of her life with a severe phobic fear of water. She became sick to her stomach if she had to stand near a pool (which she only did when treatment demanded), if she was caught in the rain, or if she drove past a lake or along the ocean shore. She developed a splitting headache every time she came in for treatment, and she literally could not look at water, even from a distance, without feeling ill. Even thinking about water caused her to have headaches and an upset stomach.

She could not recall a time in her life when she was free from this fear. I had been treating her, using systematic desensitization and R.E.T. for a year and a half, which is not at all unusual for such a deep-seated phobia, and I had so far had minimal success.

One day after learning about and studying applied kinesiology, I tried this new approach. The treatment took only about 1 1/2 minutes. When I tested her after the treatment, it appeared that she had lost her fear. She knew immediately — even before any verification by testing — that the fear was gone. My tests confirmed that she was right.

Nevertheless, I could barely believe what she was saying. In order to check this out, I brought her directly out to the pool. Always before she had backed away, terrified, but now she ran to the deep end, bent down and splashed water into her face, laughing with delight.

The following day, she reported on her first night of "freedom." That evening we had a terrible thunderstorm. I was well aware that this event would normally be an occasion of particular fear for her. But she told me she had felt a wish to stand and watch the storm over the ocean in order to give an acid test to the cure. She drove to the shore (something she had never done before, even with company), parked her car, and walked down to the dark raging water. She told me that, standing there — alone — she felt a deep inner joy. Her lifetime of fear was ended.

It was, indeed. Even her nightmares (in which she was drowning or caught in a strong surge of water) which had often, in the past, wakened her in a fit of terror did not return. This was five years ago, and there has been no recurrence.

How did I effect this "miraculous" cure?

My first thought was that, in some way, the cure might have been effected by suggestion, charisma, the "placebo effect" — or even, possibly, by some form of hypnosis. Yet, I knew that I had not hypnotized my patient, nor had I made any grand claims that the treatment I was going to give her would succeed. I had not even known if it would be even mildly successful. But since that first case, I have proven conclusively to myself that my "Five-Minute" treatment does not involve any of these elements.

The first indication that this is so comes from the high rate of success I have experienced — 85% cure. Neither suggestion nor hypnosis have ever had so high a rate of success. Also, this treatment lasts. Patients whom I treated over five years ago are still free of their phobias. The chances of a "suggestion cure" lasting are slight. Most fade either quickly or gradually, beginning almost immediately.

Just the other day, I treated a young woman for a severe phobia, which she rated at 7 to 8 on an upward scale of 10. Immediately after the treatment, I asked her to give me a number so I would know how she now felt. She would not give me a number. I kept asking her, and she responded by giggling. [Difficulty in coming up with a number after treatment is a typical good sign. There is usually no problem before the treatment.] She finally asked me how I had performed the "trick," since she didn't like to admit that she had been "taken in." Yet she could not deny that the relief was definite — and lasting. Some other patients have called my cure "witchcraft." But "witchcraft," when it is effective, is simply science that is not yet understood.

Another indication that this treatment is neither based on suggestion nor hypnosis is that I have successfully treated a number of people who not only did not have an open mind regarding what was taking place — they obviously were convinced that I was some kind of madman. If anything, in such a situation, there is a certain amount of negative suggestion that must be overcome. [Many of my successful treatments have been done in the face of obvious negative suggestion.]

There are two other indications that the success of this treatment is not due to suggestion or to charisma. 1) I have repeatedly tested these possibilities by using the cure to treat total strangers who cannot possibly have any feelings toward me as an individual and who are not "under my influence" in any way. It works just as well with such individuals as it does with my patients. Further, 2) I have taught the treatment to others, some psychologists and some interested laymen, and they have all been very successful.

It has been observed over and over again that, in any test of a new drug where half the subjects are given the drug and half a placebo, at least some of the people treated with the placebo are cured. Why? It is assumed that they believe they are getting the real medicine, and so their bodies react — and a cure is effected. This "placebo effect" is common that most people are well acquainted with it and, even though it is difficult to explain, they can accept it as being a "real" result. Which, of course, it is.

It is not surprising then, that one might wonder whether my "Five-Minute" treatment is, in reality, merely an extension of the "placebo effect." I considered that possibility myself when I first observed the dramatic effect of my cure. But I soon abandoned that idea. The "placebo effect" usually works only when the patient believes that he will be helped by the pill or treatment which he receives. That belief is essential to the cure.

My "Five-Minute" treatment follows an entirely different pattern. I have cured strangers who, all the while, I was performing the actions that effect the cure were amused, even openly skeptical of what was taking place. That is actually the opposite of what happens with the "placebo effect." Such persons *do not expect* that my treatment will help. I would estimate, in fact that over 98 percent of the patients I have treated successfully are at least actively skeptical if not hostile when they are first exposed to the unorthodox procedures. My early cures have taken place in the face of highly active negative suggestion.

I recognize that the expectations of the therapist might influence the rate of success. Yet I have always expected to be able to cure my patients, even before I began using this "Five-Minute" treatment, when my rate of success was comparable with that of other effective psychologists. I would not waste a client's time and money if I felt he was incurable.

Yet, when I began using my new cure, I wasn't sure it would work. I certainly was not prepared for its spectacular effect. I was amazed. More amazed, possibly, than my patients. When it continued to be effective — and when it became clear that the cure lasted — my confidence grew. So my present expectation of success when using the "Five-Minute" treatment is based on extensive successful experience, and not the other way around.

As I have explained earlier, I believe that a phobia is basically a natural mental defense mechanism gone wrong. It also can be described as a disruption of normal energy flow along one meridian — usually the stomach meridian (see chapter 6). Whenever a phobic is exposed to a feared situation, or even if he just thinks about it, this disruption in his energy circulation occurs.

Many phobic sufferers today have learned to mask their fears under a blanket of alcohol, or tranquilizers — both consciousness-numbing drugs. Airlines, knowing this, place the bar close to passenger-loading areas and serve a steady supply of alcohol during flight.

The problem with using such drugs is, however, twofold. Firstly, when the effect of the drug wears off, the phobia is still there — sometimes stronger than before. The subject will succumb to panic and fear again, when the object or situation that triggers the phobia reoccurs — and the reaction may be more intense than it was before. Such drugs do not cure. They only temporarily mask the problem.

Secondly, using alcohol or tranquilizers could cause a phobic to stop looking for a cure, since he might feel content with the stop-gap measure drugs provide.

We don't really know why this cure works. Yet, it is wrong to assume that because we cannot yet explain in detail just how this treatment works we dare not use it. The old comparison to electricity serves well here.

We have been "using" electricity for years now, yet even the most knowledgeable scientist cannot give a complete explanation of how and why it works. Certainly the average layperson does not even bother to concern himself with this curiousity. He "uses" electricity without worry, without feeling any hesitation. He doesn't care why it works. It is enough for him that it does.

At present, this approach to my "Five-Minute" treatment is the best we can offer a layperson. However, I am convinced that in time, when laboratory studies, especially biochemical studies, are carried out, we will understand completely the how and why of the "Five-Minute" treatment for phobias. Right now, it will have to be enough that it works.

The Testing —
General
Directions

Most people today have heard of "lie-detectors," and are aware that these electronic devices are used to determine whether a person is lying or telling the truth by examining body responses. These machines test pulse rate, perspiration, respiration rate, and blood pressure as a subject responds to questions. A sudden change in any of these factors indicates the possibility that the individual is telling an untruth. These changes vary in individuals, it is true. For example, in a child all such changes are quite small, sometimes almost unnoticeable, while in a strong man the range of responses is amplified. Though results are controversial, they still provoke much interest.

Changes are brought about by the *fact* of telling an untruth, *not by the intention* of the subject. The innovative opthamologist, Bates, reported that visual acuity decreases when a person states an untruth, even though there may be no intent to deceive.

Dr. Goodheart, in the 1960s, found that he could evaluate normal and abnormal body functions by using specific muscle tests, such as the "arm test" mentioned at the start of Chapter 3. Since that discovery, the principle of using muscle tests to evaluate body abnormalities has been broadened to include the evaluation of the nervous, vascular, lymphatic systems and cerebrospinal fluid function. It also is used to study the effects of nutrition and acupuncture. This new system of diagnosing body dysfunctions is called "applied kinesiology."

The International College of Applied Kinesiology* defines applied kinesiology as follows: "The science of applied kinesiology is an organized diagnostic approach of evaluation and physiological therapeutics organized and developed within the chiropractic profession using muscle relationships and muscle-organ relationships as determined by manual, mechanical or electronic forms of muscle testing. It allows evaluation and correction of bodily dysfunction and it aids in the prevention of disease and the promotion of health."

The testing of muscles for energy diagnosis, as carried out by doctors trained in applied kinesiology, can be very complex. However, it is possible to make us a simplified version of the test. In this version there is no equipment used, and only two people are needed — the tester and the subject.

This test, which is described by John Diamond, M.D., in his book *Behavioral Kinesiology,* is the one I use when examining my patients. It is simple and easy to perform, and can be used by any person who wishes to identify and treat his own or a friend's simple phobias. But before it is applied to any specific problem, you should master the simple techniques involved:

The test is performed in the following manner:

1) Tester and subject stand facing each other, a comfortable distance apart. The subject stands with his right arm relaxed at his side and holds out his left arm (right arm, if the

---

*International College of Applied Kinesiology, P. O. Box 680547, Park City, Utah 84068.

tester is left-handed) parallel to the shoulder. The elbow should be straight throughout the test, with the palm of the hand facing the ground.

Figure A
Test Position

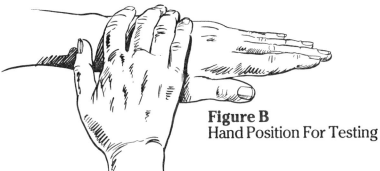

Figure B
Hand Position For Testing

2) The tester faces the subject, placing his left hand on the subject's right shoulder and his right hand on the subject's left wrist. The subject should be told that you are going to press down on his arm and he is to resist as best he can against your pressure.

3) During the test, approximately 15 pounds of pressure will be applied to the left wrist of the average adult. (To determine what 15 pounds of pressure is, place a bathroom scale on a counter or dresser which is at your shoulder height. Extend the arm you will use to exert the pressure on a subject's extended arm [see Fig. A] and press down on the scale until it reads 15. This is the pressure you will use when testing for phobias.) The intent of the tester is not to overpower the subject, but rather to recognize either a strong resistance to the pressure, a locking of the muscles, or a definite inclination to succumb to the pressure.

It is important that the tester apply the same amount of pressure each time he tests a particular person, and that he keeps his mind clear of any specific expectation as to how the test will come out. [In other words, to the best of his ability, the tester should not, before he performs the tests, decide how the subject will respond.] Once you determine that the person tests strong, stop pushing. Extended pressure will just fatigue both you and the subject.

If you are a strong person, and everyone always tests weak, you will need to adjust your pressure so that it's appropriate to the subject. You should be able to test a child by reducing the pressure and adapting yourself to his range. In like manner, you should adjust to each subject you test.

4) Testing in the clear. [This test is performed to give you, the tester, some "feel" for how your subject will react when he is not thinking of any problem.] Tell the subject to resist your pressure. Then, smoothly, apply pressure to the arm. You will

meet strong resistance. Do not try to overpower the person. Make sure he is ready before you begin; you don't want to surprise him. Tell him you are going to test and ask him to resist against your pressure as best he can. Then simply press until you feel this resistance in the shoulder muscle. When you feel it, stop.

5) To help you identify the difference between a strong and a weak resistance, first ask the subject to repeat: "My name is (fill in his correct name)." Test him as above, immediately. He will test strong. Now tell him to say: "My name is (fill in another name, not his own)." His arm will usually go down under the same pressure you exerted before.

This is the basic test. The cause of the weakness when an untruth was spoken appears to be due to the fact that when stress is created in the body (because of the untruth) the stress results in a general weakness in the body. For most people it works easily and with a definite difference between a weak and strong response. The difference, in fact, is dramatic.

However, there are some people who do not seem to respond as reliably to this test. We know that "lie-detectors" are not infallible indicators of truth, either. But since both processes work some of the time, they are, nevertheless, valuable aid, each in its own field.

I find that about 2% of the population is very difficult to test. When I encounter such a person, I ask him to drink a glass of water (the amount of water in the body seems to affect response to this test), and I test again. When even this does not clarify the subject's response, I ask him to help me judge whether he is responding weakly or strongly to my pressure.

Figure C
Arm goes down when
subject tests weak

If you are not able to distinguish a definite difference in response when you try this test, find someone else to perform the test on this subject. There are a number of circumstances in which the test will not work which we will deal with in the chapter on troubleshooting. Right now, it is important that you master the technique and feel comfortable with it before we proceed.

To continue:

6) Perform a number of tests with your subject. Tell him to think of something pleasant — something he enjoys. Test his arm. It should be strong.

7) Now have him think of something he dislikes very much. This time the arm should test weak.

8) There are other opposites you can have the subject consider.

A happy time and an unhappy time.

A person he likes and a person he dislikes.

A pretty flower and a obnoxious weed.

What is important in these different "tests" is that you learn to easily identify the strong and weak response. Each time you test using the questions suggested above, you should grow more at ease with the amount of pressure you need to apply and with discerning the response you get.

A note is needed here regarding a person who responds "weak" to a happy situation or pleasant thought and "strong" when asked to think of an unhappy situation or thought. It is a condition in which a person seems to have reversed reactions to pleasure and pain, happiness, and unhappiness.

Such a person will usually test weak if asked to say "I want to be happy," and strong if asked to say "I want to be miserable," even though he will insist that he wants to be happy and has no wish to be miserable. Many patients who come to me are reversed only in regard to their phobia. If, in your preliminary testing, you encounter a person who appears to have this reversed reaction, you must treat that condition before you try to deal with any other problem. This difficulty will be dealt with in the next chapter.

Psychological Reversal

There is not a psychotherapist practicing who has not encountered a patient who simply cannot be cured, no matter how effective the therapy ordinarily is or how diligently the patient and therapist apply themselves to the task. This resistance to treatment is a frustration to therapists and a trial to their patients. It has been called by many names, such as: *death instinct,* the *loser syndrome, self-defeating behavior,* or *negativity.* These troubled patients are called by many names: *recalcitrant patients, negative personalities, self-destructive individuals* — but their situation is always much the same. They seem to resist all help — no matter what approach is used. They claim they want to be cured — *but they do not respond* to treatment.

While I was working with an overweight woman who professed to want to be thin, I encountered this negative block. She had been dieting with little success for years. Yet, in spite of her failure to cut down on eating, she insisted that she wanted to lose weight.

Using the muscle test, I asked her to picture herself thin,

the way she said she wished to be. The result startled me. When she succeeded in picturing herself minus her extra weight, her arm tested weak.

We were both surprised. Yet, in spite of the negative results, she insisted that she did want to lose weight.

So I tried a different approach. I asked her to picture herself 30 pounds heavier than she was. Now she tested strong.

I restated the question even more directly. I had her say aloud, "I want to lose weight." The test suggested that her statement was not true.

Now I had her say "I want to gain weight." This time she tested strong. Obviously, there was a discrepancy between what she *said* she wanted and what the *tested indicated* that she wanted.

Curious, I tried this same test on six other clients who had been dieting for months or years without success. They all showed the same pattern. What they said they wanted was the reverse of what they were shown to want when I tested them using the same muscle test.

This was, certainly, not the first time I had encountered resistance to treatment. But now I had a tool with which to identify it and, possibly overcome it. To have the name of this condition also be a description of it, I called it *Psychological Reversal*.

The phenomenon of *psychological reversal* is responsible for the repeated failure of so many people to overcome their fears even though they try extensive treatments of all kinds. They appear to be impervious to healing, no matter what they do. They appear to resist cure, *even though they act as if they want to be rid of their phobias,* and *believe that they want to live without fear.*

In the case of my overweight patients, I at first considered that this weakness that appeared when I tested them and asked them to picture themselves thin was associated with a fear of sexuality. It is often assumed by both psychologists and laymen that some individuals are overweight in order to obscure their fear of sex. But when I discovered the same weakness regarding weight loss in a middle-aged, big, tough, happily married construction foreman I had to rethink that supposition. I knew this man well, and was quite confident that he harbored no fear of being slender and sexually attractive. Yet, this still left the question as to why they should test strong when they pictured themselves gaining weight.

Now I began to test all my other clients with reference to their major problems (ie: "I want to get over my anxiety attacks," "I want to get a better relationship with my wife/husband/lover," "I want to overcome my frigidity/impotence/premature-ejaculation," or "I want to be a successful and/or fine actor/singer/musician or composer." etc.) In each case, I also had the patient make a reverse statement (ie: "I do not want to get over my anxiety attacks." etc.) And each time I tested, using the arm test.

I was flabbergasted at the results of these tests. I found to my chagrin that a large number of my clients got weak when they thought of getting better and stronger when they thought of getting worse.

No wonder psychotherapy is so difficult! Looking back over the clients I had treated before my discovery of this reversal phenomenon, I realized that there are many whom I now would have labeled reversed. Their cures had been slow and painful. Yet, many of them had done well, even though it had been a hard long struggle for us both. I realized now that something had changed during the treatment of those who had been cured that permitted them, finally, to respond to the therapy I was using to rid them of their phobias. I knew that I had to find a definite, repeatable method for overcoming this roadblock on the road to health which frustrated both me and my patients.

What is Psychological Reversal?

A psychological reversal exists when a person claims he desires to achieve a specific goal but his actions and major motivation, and especially his results, are contrary to his stated goal. Superficially or outwardly he appears to be striving to achieve (in the area of his behavior where he is reversed), but he will inevitably, grossly or subtly, sabotage his own every effort.

A psychological reversal is revealed when a person who tests strong when tested in the clear has the indicator muscle go weak when he states or imagines a positive goal that he says he desires to achieve. When he states or imagines the failure or negative of that goal, he tests strong.

Testing strong on failure is required in order that the condition be considered psychological reversal. If the individual tests weak on achieving and on failing, but tests strong "in the clear," the conflict could merely be due to the stress that surrounds that particular area in his thoughts.

From a motivational standpoint, psychological reversal is a perversion of how one's system ought to work. Psychologically, reversal appears to originate when aspirations are constantly thwarted, or when an individual develops a strong sub-conscious tendency to denigrate himself and expect failure. My observations suggest that physical stress may also generate psychological reversal in an individual with a proclivity in that direction. However, whatever the origin of the condition, its effects are definite — and devastating.

If you consider that a person carries around within him an internal conditioning response system, somewhat like the Shick system for quitting smoking (where a mild stress or shock is given every time a cigarette is seen or thought about), you can then understand what a person suffering from psychological reversal is up against. He is punished with stress (goes weak) when he thinks of his avowed goal and rewarded (with strength) when he thinks of failure. A perversion, if ever there was one. Such a person is not geared for success. He is "tuned in" to failure — and repeated failure is his reward.

We all have experienced it at one time or another. We want to lose 10 pounds of excess weight, but no matter how hard we try, we just can't seem to do it. We cheat — and then forget what we did. We seem determined to sabotage our own wishes for success.

Anyone who works with people is aware that some very intelligent and seemingly highly motivated individuals fail no matter what program, method of treatment, coaching technique, educational procedure (or whatever) is used. With such chronic failures it seem likely that when a particular technique is finally successful it is because some specific technique or some special coach or doctor has managed to unwittingly correct the psychological reversal which up until that moment thwarted all attempts at cure. But it also becomes obvious that in other cases some teachers, coaches, or doctors actually may induce reversal in at least some of their patients.

Many psychologists have stated over the years that certain patients want to be ill, or want to be disturbed, or want to die, even though they actively seek help. Freud postulated a "death instinct" to account for this. Albert Ellis points out that most neurotics are self-sabotaging and self-defeating.

Religions, too, are faced with believers who, despite their professed desire to live according to the precepts of their religion, still cannot seem to do it. The problem exists among both laymen and leaders.

In Romans 7:18-20, this dilemma is presented, in a religious context, by Saint Paul.

(18) "For I know that in me (that is, in my flesh), dwelleth no good thing: for to will is present with me; but how to perform that which is good I find not.

(19) For the good that I would I do not: but the evil which I would not, that I do.

St. Paul proceeds to give an explanation for his dilemma that is accepted still today.

(20) Now if I do that I would not, it is no more I that do it, but sin that dwelleth in me.

(21) I find then a law, that, when I would do good, evil is present with me.

(22) For I delight in the law of God after the inward man:

(23) But I see another law in my members, warring against the law of my mind, and bringing me into captivity to the law of sin which is in my members.

(24) Oh wretched man that I am! Who shall deliver me from the body of this death?"

Thus, when a member of a religious group sins he can explain his "backsliding" by saying "The devil made me do it." Yet, both this common (and humorous) phrase, and the classification of "self-defeating" or "self-destructive" given to some patients by frustrated therapists, are actually no more nor less than attempts to in some way make understandable what I now have identified as *psychological reversal.*

Although psychological reversal is an all-or-nothing phenomenon, in different individuals it exists in varying degrees. For example, some people who are psychologically reversed as far as losing weight is concerned may weigh 300 pounds, none of which they can lose, and others may be in a constant struggle to drop ten or fifteen pounds and, though they never seem to add more weight than that, they still cannot reach their desired slimness.

Similarly, some reversed gamblers may simply lose a consistent but tolerable sum of money each time they gamble, while a more severely reversed individual will lose everything he owns or can borrow every time he is involved in gambling.

Dyslexia is a reading disability. Dyslexics, people suffering from a reading disorder, usually have a kind of severe psychological reversal that is very difficult and complex to treat. They should see an Applied Kinesiology* specialist.

I have, however, found that the treatment I give for psychological reversal can sometimes have a beneficial result in dealing with dyslexia. It's certainly worthwhile to persistently work to correct the psychological reversal in a dyslexic, though obviously this difficulty is far too involved to be dealt with by any but a qualified professional.

Susceptibility to Psychological Reversal

Susceptibility to psychological reversal varies greatly among individuals, and may vary widely within one individual over a period of time. I have noted that as a patient progresses in psychotherapy — as his self-awareness grows, as his self-acceptance is enhanced and (most importantly) as he improves his way of living — his tendency to reverse is greatly lessened. Psychological reversal can sometimes be induced by having a patient denigrate himself for his failure. It can

*International College of Applied Kinesiology, P.O. Box 680547, Park City, Utah 84068.

sometimes be eliminated by having same patient repeat a statement of self-acceptance.

It is important that one understand the manner in which psychological reversal works, for the automatic assumption may be that if one is "negative," he is negative toward everything. A demonstration of an exception to this natural assumption is a patient, a 38-year-old college student, who is not generally reversed. She is doing fine in all other areas of her life, and has no problem reading. However, she is *reversed only for chemistry.*

When this patient thinks about chemistry, she becomes psychologically reversed. She has trouble reading chemistry books, even though she never has trouble reading other subjects. Treating her for psychological reversal when she thought of chemistry solved her problem, and allowed her to bring her chemistry grades up to the level of her others.

I believe that there is a line between reversed and non-reversed states. Some individuals live constantly close to that line, on one side or the other, while other individuals are far removed from the line, either being solidly *allineated** (the positive state of not being reversed) or being "massively" reversed. In between those two extremes are found a continuum of points along which most people lie. Persons in this mid-area may have specific learning blocks or may frustrate any attempts at success only in specific areas of their lives.

If this is so (and all my experience and study indicates that it is), then all therapy, educational procedures, treatment procedures, methods of raising children, employee-employer relationships, love relationships, any interpersonal relationships, to be maximally effective, needs to take it into consider-

---

*I want to thank Dorothy Martin for suggesting the term "allineated" to designate the desireable state.

ation. Attention needs to be given to eliminating or reducing the degree of reversal of every individual before any therapy, education, treatment, personal instruction, work relationship, love-affair, or interpersonal relationship of any kind is established. When this is done, the possibility of success in is maximized, no matter what the endeavor.

Recognizing Psychological Reversal

Since I have identified the phenomenon of psychological reversal, I can sometimes detect in a client's manner, facial expression, attitude, or verbal responses. An obvious expression of psychological reversal is outright hostility, negativism, sarcasm or hopelessness. But some clients are more subtle in their reactions than others. Repeated failure to achieve success, with no obvious external reason for the failure, usually is a sign that the patient is reversed.

I was using a new treatment procedure on a young woman suffering from anorexia, and I was so absorbed in carrying out the procedure that I wasn't observing her as carefully as I usually do. One of the results of the treatment was not showing up. Frustrated, I repeated the procedure again — still to no avail.

Two days later, when I first awoke, I saw a client's face vividly in my mind. I leaped out of bed and shouted, "She was reversed! She was reversed!"

The next time I saw her, I asked her to repeat "I want a good life" as I tested her arm. She tested strong. When she made an opposite statement, "I want to be miserable," she tested weak. She was not reversed now, nor was she massively reversed. Then I performed what I call "retrospective testing."

I asked her to close her eyes and recall our previous session. While she kept that picture in her mind, I tested her with the two statements once more. Now she tested reversed.

When I explained what had happened, she was as relieved as I had been. After checking to make sure that she once more tested strong on the positive statement and weak on the negative one, I repeated the treatment that had not been successful on the previous session. This time it worked very well. Since that second session, this anorexic woman has been eating three meals a day — for the first time in fifteen years.

I warned her that she would have to be constantly alert to the possibility that she might slip back into psychological reversal, and showed her how to remedy it so that she would not be harmed by the condition. There are, unfortunately, many things that can cause an individual with a tendency in that direction to become psychologically reversed.

I believe that a tendency toward psychological reversal, like so many other things, may be influenced by genetics, nutritional problems, and metabolic imbalances. Psychomatic, sociological, and situational relationships, job problems, stress — all may make an individual particularly susceptible to reversal. But even someone who has no "built-in" tendency toward reversal can become reversed by the stresses of his life, by a relationship that is unsatisfactory, by his work — and/or by the people with whom he associates. A person who exists close to the line that separates psychological reversal from *normal allineated,* can slip easily into reversal if he speaks to someone who is massively reversed, or even who is reversed only toward the subject on which they converse.

In the past, I used to spend hours, weeks, and maybe even months or years, striving to overcome a client's negativisim. Now that I know what it is, I can deal with it much more quickly, temporarily returning the patient to an allineated state.

It must be remembered that treatment cannot be successful while a patient is in a state of psychological reversal. Even though the allineated state may be of brief duration, I can get on to the business of curing the phobias or other problems which brought the patient to me, often "smuggling in" the cure before my patient once more "slips back" into reversal.

These treatments are effective, even though the subject may slide back into reversal almost as soon as I finish working with him during any particular session. (The correction for psychological reversal may last for weeks or months, too, depending on circumstances, or it may last no more than two seconds. It may last some time if the subject manages to avoid reversal-producing situations and people.) Since psychological reversal is usually a condition of long-standing, it will have to be continually treated over a period of time.

Checking for Psychological Reversal

Since the test for reversal is simple, I suggest that it be used often by a person who is prone to psychological reversal, just to check on his "basic" attitude toward life. Make the statement: "I want to have a good life," and "I want to be miserable." Each time, have someone test your arm strength as described earlier. If you check strong on the first statement and weak on the second, you are *allineated*. If you react weakly to the positive statement and strongly to the negative one, then you are *reversed massively* (ie. reversed on many or most good things) — and you will need to deal with that condition.

If you are not massively reversed, but you are having trouble succeeding in some particular area of life (such as overcoming your phobias) check for a reversal in that specific area. Do this by repeating the sentence "I want to overcome my phobia," and then taking the arm test. Follow this by the statement "I want my phobia to get worse." Again test. If you respond weakly to the first statement and strongly to the second, then you are reversed *in that specific area.*

Treating Psychological Reversal

Any form of psychological reversal appears to be rooted in a deep rejection of self on the part of the individual. Reversed people do not believe they *deserve* to succeed. They consider themselves unworthy of good things and deserving of failure and unhappiness. Dr. Albert Ellis dubbed this syndrome the "worthless piece of shit" approach to life. A person suffering from this condition considers himself so valueless that he deserves no happiness or success in life.

I have found that this condition can exit in many degrees. One person may feel very positive and deserving in many areas of his life and worthless in only one specific field. Another individual may be suffering from a negative image of himself in every area of his life. The more extensive the psychological reversal, the more difficult it is to treat and, generally, the more often it needs to be dealt with.

There are several ways to correct psychological reversal. The best, which will establish the most effective and long-lasting cure, will only be discovered after systematic research. However, at this point, I can at least offer the findings which have come about as a result of my psychological practice.

The Self-Acceptance Affirmation

Practically all psychotherapists tend to promote self-acceptance in their clients. They have found that the person denigrating himself because he has problems has great difficulty in overcoming those problems. The person who accepts himself despite his problems seems to progress smoothly towards the successful resolution of those problems.

As a psychotherapist with many years of experience, I fell back on this axiom of self-acceptance when I was struggling to find a way to correct psychological reversal. I was very pleasantly surprised to find that uttering a self-acceptance statement out loud immediately corrected the reversal. Conversely, I also found that uttering a self-denigrating statement aloud would recreate the reversal, suggesting that the negativistic, repetitive self-denegration that so many people with neurotic problems engage in is a major cause of psychological reversal.

Merely uttering the positive affirmation will usually remove the psychological reversal even if the subject does not believe it. Obviously, if the person has a serious self-denigration problem, he should try to habituate himself to stating the positive and corrective affirmation and reduce the negativism as best he can. Simply repeating the positive affirmation will usually offer a significant beginning.

I have found that psychological reversal will almost always be corrected, temporarily, if the patient states with conviction *(even if he doesn't believe it)* "I profoundly and deeply accept myself with all my problems and all my short-comings." It is a good idea to repeat this phrase five times. Repeat the test and observe the results. Usually, the "cure" effected will be temporary.

The temporal nature of the correction suggests something important about reversal. The very nature of the affirmative statement suggests that the individual who is "corrected" when he repeats it is deficient in self-acceptance and denigrates himself excessively, at least in the area where he is reversed.

As I said before, it is not necessary that the subject believe what he is saying. But it certainly should be his goal to reach a point where he will be able to mean it in earnest every time he repeats it.

Obviously, self-acceptance cannot be permanently achieved through the mere verbalizing of one fine-sounding statement. But I do find that uttering this particular phrase corrects psychological reversal, and I recognize this as indicative that this particular client needs to set greater self-acceptance as one of his theraputic goals. The patient, too, can see the importance of self-affirmation and the need for him to increase his own feeling of value. There must be consistent follow-up that supports him as he works toward this goal, and so, in subsequent sessions we pursue this objective.

I must now return to what I said earlier (in chapter 3) regarding the treatment that I started using after studying applied kinesiology. To reinforce the effect of the positive avowal (I profoundly and deeply accept myself with all my problems and all my shortcomings) tap the side of one hand with the finger tips of the other (see Figures D & E). This will correct the blockage in the meridian in which psychological reversal is centered. We will call the treatment spot for this meridan *the psychological reversal spot.*

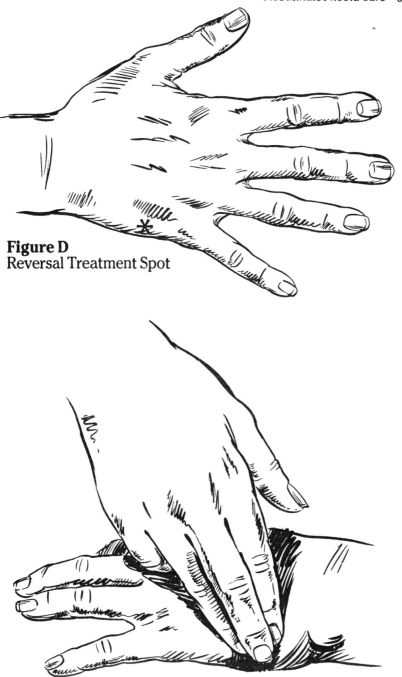

Figure D
Reversal Treatment Spot

Figure E
Reversal Treatment

To locate the exact spot to be tapped, make a fist with your right hand and hold it palm down over your lap. The spot you want to tap in on the outer edge of your hand (on the edge of the palm) just behind and lateral to the knuckle of the little finger.

Using two or three fingers (index and next 2) of the opposite hand, tap that spot vigorously 35 times. (You may undo the fist — that was just needed to make the knuckle visible.) Repeat procedure with the other hand. For an individual working by himself, the affirmation, combined with a tapping of the tips of the fingers of one hand on the fleshy part of the other hand between the little finger and the wrist, should be enough to correct reversal.

Another effective treatment for psychological reversal is an herbal remedy called "Rescue,"* which was discovered by Edward Bach, a British physician (who has a full line of herbal remedies that are available in many health food stores). The particular blend of herbs in "Rescue" I found to be of use in bringing an individual back into an allineated condition. This liquid should be squirted into the mouth (a very small amount at a time), and then held for a short time in the mouth before swallowing while the subject thinks about the area in which he is reversed. One more thing must be said regarding the meridian in which psychological reversal is located. Psychological reversal often indicates a weakness in this meridian, and so, after the treatment has successfully eliminated the psychological reversal, I recommend that "Rescue" be ingested in the above manner *once every waking hour* until allineation has been stabilized.

I repeat (because this is a point that often discourages people) that psychological reversal may return quickly after

---

*Write to: Ellon Bach USA, Inc., P.O. Box 320, Woodmere, NY 11598, if you cannot find it in your area.

the first treatment, and possibly many times again, especially if it is deeply entrenched. So the corrections procedures must be repeated often before any permanence results.

Note that I feel that the existence of psychological reversal in an individual is *not* proof that he is sabotaging his cure. I am convinced that psychological reversal, like phobias, is a condition resulting from inner imbalance, over which a person has little control.

Yet, many psychologists blame patients who seem to resist treatment. They consider that this is conscious "self-sabotage," and some even directly accuse their patients of this "crime."

This approach, I feel, is a mistake. A patient who is psychologically reversed is not necessarily *deliberately* sabotaging his own cure. Only if a patient still refuses to accept treatment after he is made aware of his reversal, or refuses to correct his psychological reversal, can he possibly be accused of being deliberately self-destructive. I feel that a patient cannot justly be accused of the "crime" of self-destruction unless a conscious decision is made by him to refuse to correct his psychological reversal once he understands it.

Massive Reversal

Soon after my discovery of psychological reversal, I found some clients who were reversed, not only in the area where they were seeking treatment, but were reversed on everything good or desirable in life. These people tested weak on anything good and tested strong on anything bad.

I test routinely for this by having the client say "I want to have a good life," and "I want to be miserable," while using the muscle-indicator test described in chapter four. These vague, general statements are effective in revealing massive reversal. Individuals who are particularly susceptible to this condition, can be "thrown into it" by the slightest form of stress, upset, or even mild self-beration, though many are constantly in this state.

There are some massively reversed individuals who are not reversed in certain delimited areas. I was lecturing to a group of actors some time ago and, among those who volunteered to serve as subjects was a man who was reversed in every area in which I tested him. His teacher suspected that he was not reversed in regard to acting, and suggested that I test on this. Much to my surprise, the instructor was right. This basically negative man showed himself to be very "positive" toward acting and, according to his teacher, was very good in that field. I have also seen some others who, though massively reversed, showed some areas of allineation.

A good example of what I call a massive reversal was displayed by a patient, George, who I treated during the period just before I began to incorporate applied kinesiology into my work. He was negative about everything. He complained that he was "getting nowhere" with therapy (though he continued to come for treatments). He was unsuccessful in his business life, his personal life was in a shambles. He made no positive moves — nor did he seem capable of looking at anything positively. I was constantly frustrated. He was, surely, "self-defeating," "self-destructive."

Then I solidified my procedures for testing and treating, using the methods described in this book. I began at once to tackle his psychological reversal. At first, I could only achieve temporary periods during which I could "slip in" a cure for one of his phobias or fears before he went back into reversal once more.

Immediately, he began to improve. We established a

regular regimen for treating his reversal (mentioned above), and gradually his life began to change. Now he is, literally, a "new man." He is successful in his work, he is dating regularly, and he has informed me that he has found a woman with whom he intends to establish a "relationship." His phobias are gone. Clearly, once we were able to correct his reversal, he was able to benefit from therapy, and all the other aspects of his life fell into place.

I recently worked with a man, suffering from anxiety and a number of phobias, who has been in therapy for 18 years. During all this time, he has basically received no help that actually rids him of his problems. Rather, he has had a series of drugs prescribed which kept him in a state of constant partial numbness. I found him to be massively reversed. For him, I advised hourly doses of "Rescue," plus almost constant repetitions of the positive affirmation phrase. With his physician's help and guidance, he gradually withdrew from the medications.

It is interesting to note that when I first asked him to repeat the positive statement of self-acceptance, he could not remember it, even repeating it immediately after me. But when, to clinically induce psychological reversal, I had asked him to repeat an equally long phrase of a negative nature, he repeated it word-for-word without my prompting. I find this phenomenon occurring frequently when I treat psychologically reversed patients.

Summary

What is important is to remember that psychological reversal can be overcome temporarily, usually by the simple act of positive affirmation mentioned above. The "fixing" will permit treatment of the phobia. And the treatment of the phobia will last, even though you slip again into psychological reversal. I suggest that before you try any treatment, you always check for reversal, so that it will not block the treatment.

It is essential that the individual repeat the vocalization of the affirmation many times — including the last half "with all my problems and with all my shortcomings." Alcoholics Anonymous, which has an excellent record in working with alcoholics has all members introduce themselves by saying "My name is ——— and I'm an alcoholic." This wisely programs self-acceptance with the problem. Self-acceptance based on delusion and distortion will be defeated by reality — and this will result in the very problem neurotics face.

One more point. It may happen that a subject tests strong on both "I want to have a good life" and "I want to be miserable." If this happens, it indicates that *both the tester and the subject* are reversed. Before continuing, both of you should repeat the positive statement of self-acceptance, tapping the side of the hand at the same time, as described earlier in this chapter.

Testing
For Fears
And Phobias

When you are comfortable with the muscle test and have a good understanding of reversal and its role in treatment, continue on to the next step, testing for fears and phobias.

1. Ask the subject to think of some fear or a phobic object or situation. It isn't necessary for the person to "get into" the fear to where he has obvious physical reactions to it. Just holding it in his mind is enough. *It is worth noting that you do not need to be told what the phobia or fear is in order for you to treat it.* The subject can thus maintain privacy if he wishes.

2. While the subject is thinking of the fear, test his arm strength as described in chapter four. The muscle will go weak. If it doesn't, check for reversal.

3. Now have the subject place his fingers of his right hand against his stomach — approximately 3 inches above the navel. (Remember, if the tester is left handed, all these directions will be reversed.) I call this area test point number 1.

4. While the subject is thinking about the fear or phobia and touching his stomach, test again. Now the arm will probably test strong. It will continue to test strong for as long as the fingers on the right hand touch the stomach area.

Figure F
Test Point #1

This test determines the precise area of energy weakness that is connected with that specific fear. I have found that the energy problem of 95% of all fears and phobias is localized in the stomach area. Another point where a few phobias seem localized is test point 2, which is located at the point illustrated below: If touching the stomach does not result in the arm testing strong then have the subject touch test spot 2 and that will usually result in a strong test. (Test spot 2 is to the side —either right or left depending on whether the tester is left or right-handed — on the last rib.)

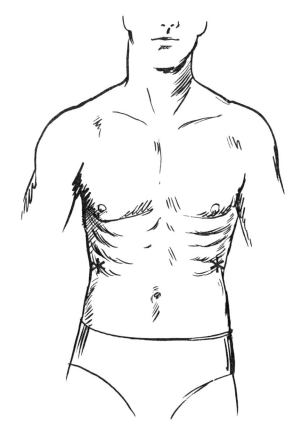

Figure G
Test Points #2

If a muscle tests weak and you touch the proper point —
the muscle will then test strong. This is called " therapy local-
ization" in applied kinesiology.

You have now found one phobia — maybe your friend is
willing to speak of it to you, and maybe he prefers to keep his
silence. Except that your curiosity may not be satisfied, there
is no difficulty, either way. Once you know a phobia, and have
ascertained which test spot it is centered in, you can proceed
to treatment.

The
Treatment*

You have tested your subject and isolated one specific phobia which he wished to have cured. You have made certain that he is not psychologically reversed.

Earlier, we spoke of the relationship between body imbalance and the existence of phobias. Now we will again consider this situation. If energy flow is disrupted in any part of the body, whether it is the cause of a phobia or the result, the energy imbalance can be treated by tapping on some point along the meridian that is disrupted.

This is why you had to test with the subject touching the stomach. You want to be sure that the phobia is related to the stomach areas before you begin treating that energy point.

Before you do anything else, ask your subject to rate the discomfort cause by this phobia — *while he is thinking about it* — on a scale from one to ten, ten being the most painful. Remember that number. It will help you and your subject recognize that he is improved when the treatment is completed. A guide for this evaluation follows.

*A summary of all "Five-Minute" phobia treatment steps is provided at the end of the book in the Summary/Workbook section.

10) The discomfort is the worst it can possibly be. I can't tolerate it. It puts me in a panic.

9) Discomfort is very close to intolerable.

8) My fear is very severe.

7) Fear is severe.

6) Fear is very uncomfortable.

5) Fear is uncomfortable, but I can stand it.

4) Fear is noticeable and bothersome, but I can stand it.

3) I feel a slight degree of fear, but I am totally in control.

2) I'm rather calm, quite relaxed, with no fear.

1) I am perfectly calm — totally relaxed.

Make a note where your subject rated his discomfort.

A small percentage of phobics get very upset when they merely *think* about their phobia. These are the people who are aware that they are cured immediately after treatment because there is such a radical change in how they feel when they *think* about their phobia.

The majority of phobics, even though the phobia may be severe, don't feel upset if they only *think* about it.

This group will not know they are cured until they encounter the reality of their phobia at some time after treatment.

(Try to find a subject, at least for your first attempts at using this treatment, who either is upset when thinking about his phobia or who suffers from claustrophobia, since closets are rather ubiquitous, or some other phobia that can easily be tested immediately after treatment. This immediate feedback will give you confidence when you continue.)

Now You Can Proceed
With The Treatment

You recall that when we corrected psychological reversal, one method used was to tap repeatedly on the fleshly part of the side of the hand, just below the knuckle at the base of the little finger. You will do the same sort of tapping again, but in different locations. (See Figures H, I, I.a, and J.)

I find that almost all phobias involve the stomach area. The only exceptions I have found so far are the fear of spiders and some aspects of flying, which involved phobia test point and treatment point # 2 in the cases I have treated.

When the subject's resistance to the tester's pressure is strong before he is asked to think about his fear and weakens when he is thinking of his fear, and is not strengthened when he touches the test point number 1, then try having him touch test point number 2. Also, remind him to keep resisting each time you test. Sometimes subjects forget that it is necessary.

When the arm strengthens, proceed with the treatment, tapping the appropriate "treatment point" (2nd toes & eye sockets for test spot 1 and fifth rib up and big toes for test spot 2) for the area that was affected. If you have determined that the stomach area is involved (by testing the subject while he thinks of his phobia and touches his stomach with his left hand and his previously weak arm thereby strengthens), then proceed to treat the energy imbalance as follows:

Have the subject remove his shoes and socks. Tap firmly on the second toes (next to the big toe), just behind the nail, on the side furthest from the big toe. Have him *think of his fear or phobia* while you tap that spot on both feet. You should repeat the tapping approximately thirty-five times on each foot, but you can tap on both feet at the same time. This should take about thirty seconds.

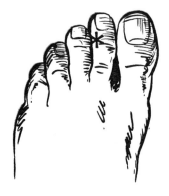 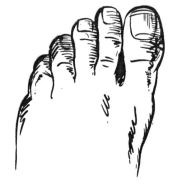

Figure I
Treatment Point for
Test Point #1

Figure I.a
Treatment Point for
Test Point #2

If you are in a situation where the removal of shoes and socks is impractical, the same tapping may be done with the tips of the index fingers and the middle fingers at the edge of the bone of the eye sockets, just beneath and center of the eye. This is another phobia treatment point. However, since this area is far more sensitive and subject to bruising, the tapping should be done with less vigor. It should, however, be continued for the same length of time (30 seconds or 35 times). *Remember that the subject must be thinking about his phobia when you do the tapping.*

Repeat the arm test and make sure your subject is strong while thinking of his phobia. Check again for psychological reversal and if your subject is allineated he/she should be cured. Ask him/her, to quantify how he feels on the ten-point scale of discomfort.

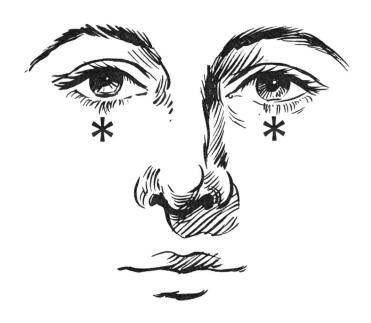

Figure J
Treatment Point for
Test Point #1

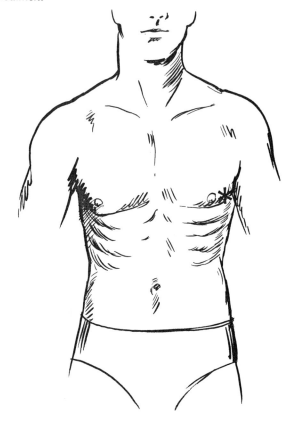

Figure H
Treatment Points for
Test Point #2

That is usually all there is to the treatment. It seems too simple, considering the trouble the phobia can *and has* caused. But simple as it is, it still is powerfully effective.

This treatment (tapping the toes or just below the eyes while the subject thinks of his phobia) cures about 85% of my cases. However, if there is still substantial fear present (above 2 on the 1 to 10 scale), you may try the following for either test spot 1 or 2:

1) Eye closure test. Test the subject after the toe-tapping treatment. Remember that he should think about his phobia while you perform the test. He should test strong. If he still feels the fear, test for psychological reversal. Ask him to say "I want to be over this fear," and after testing for that reaction, test with the statement, "I want my fear to be worse."

If he is not reversed, but the fear persists, have him *close his eyes* and concentrate on the phobia. Test him again. See if he now tests weak. If so, have subject keep *eyes closed* while you tap the back of both of his hands (one at a time) 35 times between the pinky and the ring finger as shown in Figure K. If the subject tests strong, proceed to eye-open test.

2) Test again, *with eyes open.* This is to take care of any possibility that your subject closed his eyes automatically while thinking of the phobia during treatment. If the arm goes down easily when the subject has his eyes open and is thinking about his phobia, proceed with the following treatment:

Have subject keep *eyes open* while you tap the back of his hand as above.

If arm resists strongly, the subject is okay for this condition, and should be tested under the following conditions, and treated appropriately.

Additional Treatments

If there is still substantial fear* remaining after the preceding treatments (2 or more on the 10 point scale) then test and treat as follows (for either test spot 1 or 2). It's important to note that if the subject tests weak for any of the following conditions, he or she should be treated for that condition as

---

* Remember, the patient may not actually feel fear when merely *thinking* of the phobia. Fear may, however, still be present. In which case, the additional treatments should be applied.

explained below. If, however, the subject tests strong, proceed to next condition.

Humming

Think of the phobia and hum a tune simultaneously. The tune, it can be anything such as "Yankee Doodle" which most people know, should be hummed aloud. Test while doing this. Some people think that they go weak on this because of the multiplicity of tasks but that is not the reason. You will see that after the treatment you can perform all of this with ease.

If an arm that is normally strong goes weak when subjected to the above task then treat as follows.

Tap the back of the hands 35 times as indicated in Figure K while having subject hum aloud and think of his phobia.

Test again while having subject hum and think of phobia, and see if arm is strong. If it now is strong and there is still some fear left then go on with further tests and treatments. Once the

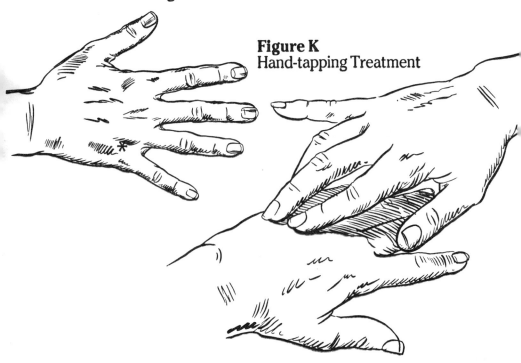

Figure K
Hand-tapping Treatment

fear is gone, of course, there is no need to treat further unless in the unlikely event that the fear should return. When this does happen, it is rare, it is usually due to a persistently recurring psychological reversal.

If the fear is very persistent and the subject tests strong to all the tests be sure to re-check for psychological reversal because, if the subject is reversed he will give a falsely strong reading. If not reversed, go on to additional treatments.

Multiplication

Now test while the subject is thinking of the phobia and doing the multiplication tables out loud. If the test is weak, tap the spot indicated in Figure K 35 times on the back of each hand while the subject is multiplying and thinking of the phobia you are treating.

Test again while subject does multiplication out loud and thinks of phobia. He should now test strong after the treatment.

If the subject tested strong for humming and then tested weak on multiplication then it is a good idea after treatment to go back again and re-test for humming. Sometimes a humming weakness will show up only after the multiplication weakness is corrected. If that happens treat accordingly. If fear persists, proceed to Eye Position treatment.

Eye Position

Have subject think of phobia and while holding head still (many people move their head when asked to move only their eyes) move the eye into a down and left position (see Figure L) and test. If arms goes weak then treat as follows.

While thinking of phobia and keeping eyes in the down left position tap vigorously the spot on the hand indicated (see Figure K) about 35 times on each hand.

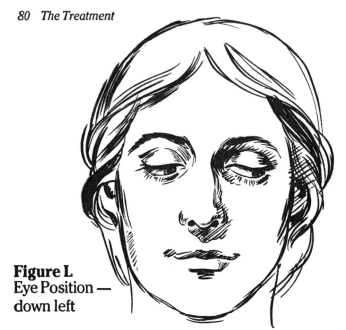

Figure L
Eye Position —
down left

If the subject doesn't go weak in the down left eye position then have him think of the phobia and put eyes in a down right (see Figure M) position (a subject usually goes weak on only one of the two positions not both). If he goes weak now treat the spot indicated in Figure K by tapping it 35 times while the subject holds his eyes in the down right position and thinks of his phobia. Continue on to Eye Roll if subject still feels fear.

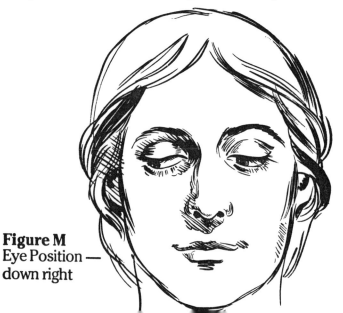

Figure M
Eye Position —
down right

Eye roll

Have subject think of phobia and roll his eyes in the direction indicated in Figure N to the left, counter clockwise and test. If the subject tests weak then tap the spot (about 35 times on each hand) indicated in Figure K while he rolls eyes in the same direction and thinks of his phobia.

Figure N
Eye Roll — to the left
(counter-clockwise)

Have subject think of phobia and roll his eyes in the opposite direction (see Figure O), to the right, clockwise and test. If weak on this have subject think of phobia and tap the spot about 35 times on each hand indicated in Figure K while subject continually rolls eyes in that direction. Subject should test strong after treatment while repeating eye position or movement and while thinking of phobia.

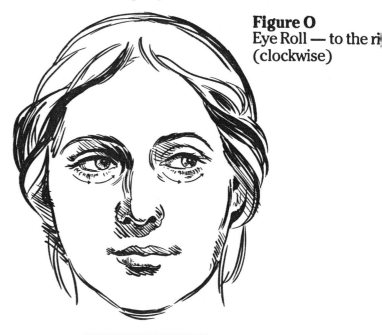

Figure O
Eye Roll — to the ri
(clockwise)

Treating Remaining Fear

After completing the above treatment, some fear may remain (3 or 2 on a 10-point scale). Though this may be quite acceptable, it may be possible to eliminate this remaining fear completely. Ask subject to rate fear again on the 10-point scale. Have him or her tune into the remaining fear and test again. If arm goes down, have person touch the test point (stomach or side) that he or she originally responded to. If while touching that point the arm is strong, treat again using original treatment on corresponding treatment point. After treatment, ask for another 1 to 10 rating. In most cases it will have gone down further, often to 1.

It's important to note that if fear remains and arm does not go down during test, the possibility of reversal should be examined.*

You may now go on to the verification. The treatment is complete.

Verification

You can readily see that a subject might have a difficult time recognizing that anything has happened to him, even though he might "feel better." Certainly, he (and possibly you, if you haven't done this before) will have serious doubts that the phobia or fear is, indeed, gone.

The best way to confirm the cure is to test it immediately. There are two ways available.

1. The first way of testing requires that you recall how high the subject rated his phobia before you tested him. Now, after the treatment, ask him to think of the phobia and rate it again. He will often have trouble coming up with a number, but when he does, he will generally rate it lower. [Remember: Some people react very quickly to this cure — others are slow reactors, and may need a few minutes before the cure takes full effect.] This is the least satisfactory methods of testing a

---

*Psychological reversal may occur at anytime in some people. People who do not test positively for reversal early on, may do so later in the process. This is why it is important to test for reversal throughout the treatment stages.

cure, since you cannot test the reaction of the subject in a "real life" situation. It does not confront the "real" issue. How is the subject going to react when he once again encounters a situation that has always, in the past, brought on a phobic reaction?

2. The second and most conclusive method of testing is to present the subject with the object or situation that has in the past caused phobic reactions. I did this with the woman who feared water, bringing her face to face with a phobic-creating situation. And in that confrontation lay the drama. She did not need reinforcing again, after that spectacular experience. She *knew* the phobia was gone.

Another example comes to mind. I met a woman at the foot of the aerial tramway up to the top of San Jacinto Mountain, just outside of Palm Springs, California. She wanted very much to take the ride — but she was terrified of heights, and dared not enter the tram. I treated her right there, before we boarded, and I went with her to the top. I was able to observe that the phobia was gone, for she enjoyed not only the view from the top of the mountain, but even took pleasure in the ride up.

It is important that you remember that there is always a reason when someone is not responsive to treatment. Because this treatment is so new, we do not yet know all the possible explanations for a failure, nor even all the reasons that may compound in one single case.

I have found that the most common difficulty resulting in unsuccessful treatment is a recurring psychological reversal. In such cases, the treatment (both for reversal and for the phobia) needs to be repeated as often as is necessary.

Occasionally a problem arises because some aspect or nuance of a phobia has not been thought about by the subject during the treatment. Often this results because the subject himself is not even aware of this nuance. Whatever the cause, the result is that the specific nuance that is omitted from consciousness during the treatment is not treated, leaving the possibility that the fear may be aroused at some later time, though this is a rare event.

There might be some evidence of this when you ask your subject to rate his feelings, now that the cure has taken place. He will indicate that he feels "about a four." He may even rate his feelings as high as five. If this happens, I recommend the following procedure:

After you have   performed   the tests   listed   , check your subject once more for psychological reversal. If he is now reversed, treat first for this difficulty. Then ask the subject to think of every aspect of his phobia that he might have forgotten the first time you performed the cure. While he has these nuances and aspects in mind, repeat the treatments. When it is completed, test again. Now you will usually find that the subject rates his feelings far lower — maybe even as low as one.

Treating Yourself

Although, it is preferable to undergo the testing and treatment with another person, if you are alone or prefer not to include another person in the treatment you can treat yourself as follows.

Correcting Psychological Reversal

First you want to clear yourself of a possible psychological reversal. Remember that if you are in a psychologically reversed state, you cannot benefit from any kind of treatment. If you treat yourself for psychological reversal and in fact you are not reversed the treatment is harmless, it will not create a reversal where there was none. To be safe, therefore, assume that you are reversed and treat for it.

Think of the phobia or irrational fear that you wish to overcome and state out loud while thinking of that fear, "Even

though I have this fear I deeply and profoundly accept myself."
Repeat this five times.

While vocalizing this self-acceptance affirmation tap yourself vigorously in the spot indicated in Figures D & E. Tap spot on each hand about 35 times.

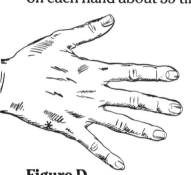

Figure D
Reversal Treatment Spot

Figure E
Reversal Treatment

If you have obtained the Bach remedy "Rescue" put a few drops in your mouth and hold it there while you think of overcoming your fear. After holding it in your mouth for about 30 seconds and thinking of your fear, swallow it.

Any one of these three reversal corrections should be sufficient but you may wish to use all three.

Phobia Treatments

Establish a point on the ten point scale that you will feel best represents the degree of fear you feel when thinking about this particular phobia.

> 10) The discomfort is the worst it can possibly be. I can't tolerate it. It puts me in a panic.
>
> 9) Discomfort is very close to intolerable.
>
> 8) My fear is very severe.
>
> 7) Fear is severe.
>
> 6) Fear is very uncomfortable.
>
> 5) Fear is uncomfortable, but I can stand it.
>
> 4) Fear is noticeable and bothersome, but I can stand it.
>
> 3) I feel a slight degree of fear, but I am totally in control.
>
> 2) I'm rather calm, quite relaxed, with no fear.
>
> 1) I am perfectly calm — totally relaxed.

There is no necessity to labor over this evaluation, just give your best impression. Remember you and only you are the world's leading authority on how you feel. You will repeat this evaluation after you complete the treatment in order to evaluate the effectiveness of the treatment. If you are one who gets very upset by merely thinking of the phobic situation you will get immediate verification of the power of the treatment. If you don't get upset when just thinking of the phobia you will have to wait until you are in the phobic situation.

It is typical after a successful treatment to have difficulty coming up with a number to quantify the anxiety. Do the best you can. Probably the main reason for this difficulty is that the former fear is no longer a fear and is, thereby, hard to think about.

Some beginners with this approach sometimes think that the fear reduction is due to the distraction provided by the treatment. But anyone who has tried to use distraction for their severe fears (almost everyone has tried it at sometime with little or no success) can tell you how inadequate it generally is. A severe fear is quite consuming of one's attention. In addition to the inadequacy of distraction the treatment itself requires your attention to be continually on the fear. The treatment, in other words, requires you to keep thinking of the fear even if you were trying to distract yourself.

When one has a severe fear for any length of time it is very strange indeed to be able to think about the feared object or situation without the simultaneous occurrence of high anxiety. This is especially true when the change takes place so suddenly as it does in this treatment.

When carrying out the treatment 1 or treatment 2 keep your eyes open while thinking of the phobia to simplify the procedures.

Treatment One

Since you are doing this alone no diagnosis is done so assume that the test spot is, the most common type — #1.

While thinking of the fear tap under the eyes; about thirty-five times each eye (See Figure J). You may supplement this treatment by tapping on your second toes (See Figure I). Tap thirty-five times on the toes of each foot while thinking of the fear.

If we are dealing with the test spot 1 and you didn't get reversed again you should experience a dramatic reduction in the fear at this point. Re-evaluate your fear on the ten point scale and come up with a number that best represents the

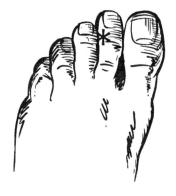

Figure I
Treatment Point for
Test Point #1

Figure J
Treatment Point for
Test Point #1

level of your fear as you experience it now. If you have a severe fear but only experience the fear when exposed to the actual situation you will have to wait until you are in that situation to discover the outcome of the treatment. If you still experience a fear of 2 or higher on the 10 point scale you can most likely benefit from further treatment. No matter how bad the fear is you should be able to get it within a most comfortable range with the series of treatments outlined here. If you do experience a high degree of anxiety than I recommend that, if possible, you stop the exposure to the situation until you get the fear down further through additional treatment. You should be able to be exposed to the formerly upsetting situation in comfort. You should not have to suffer. If you are unable to interrupt the situation, for example, if you are phobic for flying and you are airborne then do your best to repeat the treatments.

If you experience no difference in the fear and you have repeatedly corrected the psychological reversal then it is possible that your phobia is of the rarer type 2.

The most common problem that I encounter in my work with severe phobics is a persistently recurring psychological reversal. Keep this in mind if you are running into trouble.

Treatment Two

If you have treated for reversal and there is no reduction in the fear from treatment spots 1 then treat for test spots 2 (big toe and 5th rib). Phobias associated with test spot 2 are far more infrequent than those associated with test spot 1, but they do occur.

Tap 35 times on the treatment spots while thinking of the phobia. See Figures I.a and H.

If the fear is improved but not completely gone then the following series of procedures will usually bring the degree of fear down further. These procedures are equally applicable to test spots 1 and 2.

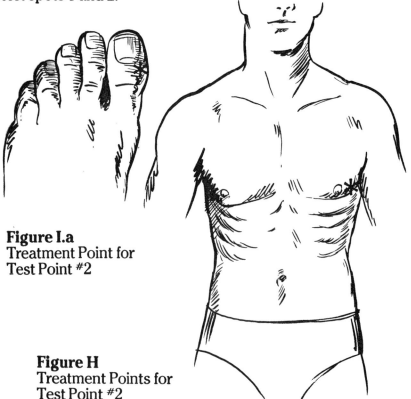

Figure I.a
Treatment Point for
Test Point #2

Figure H
Treatment Points for
Test Point #2

Eyes Closed Tapping

Think of your fear, close your eyes and tap the back of your hand as indicated in Figure K 35 times. Do each hand while keeping eyes closed and thinking of phobia.

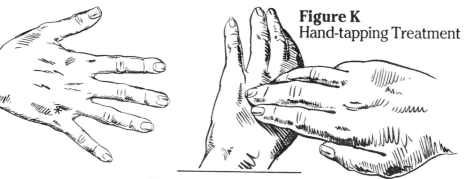

Figure K
Hand-tapping Treatment

Eyes Open Tapping

Think of your fear and while holding your eyes open and thinking of your fear tap the spot indicated in Figure K 35 times on each hand.

Humming

Tap the spot indicated in Figure K 35 times on each hand while humming (out loud, if possible) and thinking of fear. Any tune such as "Yankee Doodle" will do.

Multiplication

Think of your fear and do multiplication (out loud if possible) such as 3 x 2 = 6 etc. while you tap 35 times on each hand the spot indicated in Figure K.

Eye Positions

Hold your head still and put your eyes in a down and left position while thinking of your phobia. See Figure L. While doing this tap vigorously in the spot on the back of the hand indicated in Figure K. Use two fingers and tap for about 35 times on each hand while thinking of your phobia.

Now put your eyes in a down and right position, see Figure M, and while thinking of your phobia tap the same spot for 35 times on each hand. Keep your eyes in the given position until the tapping is finished.

While thinking of your phobia whirl your eyes in the direction indicated in Figure N to the left, counter-clockwise and continue to do that while you tap on the same spot on each hand as indicated in Figure K.

Now whirl them in the direction indicated in Figure O to the right, clockwise and tap the same spot on both hands

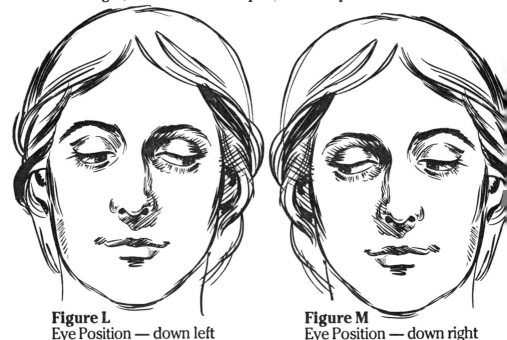

Figure L
Eye Position — down left

Figure M
Eye Position — down right

while thinking of your phobia and continuing to whirl them in the same direction until the tapping is finished.

Remember that the phobia treated by the above procedures is the phobia that you are thinking about while you are doing the treating. It doesn't matter if you really get into it or not as long as the intention to think of that specific phobia is there. Only this phobia will be treated. All the treatments must be repeated for each separate phobia. Curing one does not cure another separate phobia.

If you seem to be having difficulty intersperse reversal corrections between all of the above procedures.

If your phobia is still present have someone read the book and test you so you can isolate the specific obstruction and treat for that.

In the event that none of the above works and you want to locate a professional who is familiar with these procedures contact me at the address provided.

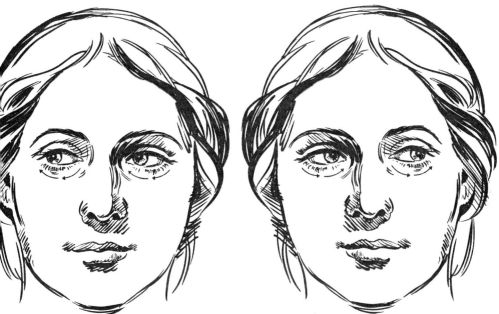

Figure N
Eye Roll — to the left
(counter-clockwise)

Figure O
Eye Roll — to the right
(clockwise)

Treating
Complex
Fears

Subconscious fears are often involved when an individual has a compound phobia such as *agoraphobia,* or suffers from a physical-psychological problem like *anorexia* or *bulimia.* At first view, these seem very complicated cases. However, it is generally possible for the phobic aspects of these difficulties to be treated by the "Five-Minute" treatment, and to have such cures be effective.

These conditions, where phobias result in actual physical illness, or where the illness contributes to the phobia, sometimes appear to be totally physical in nature. But they actually include a compound of many fears, some of which have never even been recognized by the subject.

In any compound phobia or in a situation where unconscious fears or phobias are accompanied by actual physical symptoms (as *agoraphobia* is often accompanied by hypoglycemia), the "Five-Minute" treatment can be used to eliminate individual fears, one at a time (like fear of leaving one room, fear of leaving the house, etc), so that the patient can seek help for the physical conditions that afflict him. The treatment will have no negative effects on the physical aspects of the problem, though it may sometimes cause them to be less severe. The basic thing to remember is that *this treatment does not cause harm.* Therefore, though it may be ineffective if done incorrectly or if the patient is psychologically reversed, it will never damage the patient.

The best way to identify these hidden fears is to use the arm test while having the patient make a series of statements and checking him with the arm test. I will demonstrate this procedure with a patient who suffers from agoraphobia.

Agoraphobia

I believe that if the "Five-Minute" treatment is applied in the early stages of the development of Agoraphobia, we can eliminate or greatly reduce the development of this condition in prone individuals.

Begin with the obvious. Test the arm when the subject says "I want to live a happy, fulfilling life." If the subject is not reversed, he should test strong to this statement.

Now have him say "I want to be miserable." He should test weak to this statement. If the reverse reaction appears when these two statements are made, you will first have to treat the subject for reversal (see Chapter Five). Then you can continue with the testing.

Now you must proceed through a series of questions designed to identify the individual fears. Again, begin with the obvious. If your subject is fearful of leaving her room, begin with that. When the fear is identified, treat it with the "Five-Minute" treatment.

As soon as the cure is completed, test! Ask the subject to go with you into another room of the house. If that move is made easily, you know the first fear has been eliminated. Move gradually from one fear to the other, trying not to skip around. In other words, don't leap from treating the fear to leave a room to dealing with fear of crowded shopping malls. Move gradually up the scale fears until you reach the big ones. Use the "Five-Minute" treatment in conjunction with a systematic desensitization program, attacking the weakest fears first and working up through those that are most overwhelming.

Remember to check periodically for pyschological reversal, since it is possible that a subject may slip into it without your recognizing it.

Free-Floating Anxiety

It is estimated that about ten million Americans suffer from *anxiety neurosis,* or *free-floating anxiety.* Professor Ferris N. Pitts, Jr., of the Washington University School of Medicine reported recently that about 10 to 30 percent of the patients of most general practitioners suffer from free-floating anxiety. He also found indications that there is a hereditary predisposition to this problem.

Free-floating anxiety is actually an anomaly. It would appear to be an extremely complex phobic condition, since it is impossible to isolate any specific problem, object or situation that generates the fear. Yet, in my practice, I have found that my "Five-Minute" treatment is very effective in dealing with this difficulty. In fact, I usually find that a patient suffering from free-floating anxiety will come to me rating his discomfort at ten (on the scale I mentioned earlier, in which ten is the most extreme pain and zero no pain at all) and will, after the cure, rate his discomfort at two or one, or even at zero.*

In treating specific phobias, the subject is told to focus his thoughts on the object or situation that frightens him. In treating free-floating anxiety, the tester and subject can simply focus on the feeling of anxiety and discomfort. Such a generalized focus works perfectly well when there is no object with which the tester and subject can deal.

However, one difference will soon be noted. When treating a specific phobia, one treatment usually effects a permanent cure. If the fear being treated is generalized, it may be necessary to *repeat the treatment more than once,* each time bringing the level of fear down, so he may start by feeling high anxiety, discover after the first treatment that he now feels generally keyed up and nervous, then, after a second treatment feels vaguely uneasy, and finally gets to where he feels no uneasiness at all.

In treating a patient who suffered from a number of fears, as well as from general anxiety, I found it necessary to repeat the treatment more than once. It seemed that the patient was not able to concentrate on all of his fears at one time. The second time I performed the treatment, I had him think of "all the fears he had not thought of the first time." Even though he was not consciously aware of what he was doing, apparently his sub-conscious mind carried out my order on a sub-conscious level. This time all his fears were gone.

----

*Caution: If you have been taking medication to reduce your anxiety *do not* suddenly stop because your anxiety has gone. It is very important to get medical advice on how to withdrawal from the medication.

Insomnia

Insomnia can have many causes. Most of us experience insomnia occasionally, when we are "geared up" over some highly anticipated event that lies ahead, or when we are particularly disturbed about some specific occurrence in the past. Insomnia may be the result of stress, or loneliness. It may develop after a loved one has died, or during the break-up of a romantic attachment. Such temporary insomnia usually is not the cause of much concern. When the situation changes, the insomnia disappears.

But some people suffer severely from insomnia. They may not be able to sleep at all unless they use drugs. Sometimes, such a habitual insomniac may be suffering from *apnea,* a physical condition in which, during sleep, one occasionally, momentarily, stops breathing. It is more common among men than women. A person suffering from this affliction usually recovers the ability to breath before a problem develops, but if he is aware that he has this problem, a man may resist sleep, for fear he may die in his sleep. However, often this fear is not articulated. This type of insomniac simply knows he "can't get to sleep."

This form of insomnia is long-lasting. Maybe the subject has learned to "get around it" by using drugs, or by taking catnaps when fatigue is so great it cannot be ignored, but it remains a problem for years unless treated.

The existence of apnea and the fear it engenders can be discovered if the right questions are asked during testing. Begin, as with any problem, by testing "in the clear." Then I advise having the subject make four statements (testing each one as soon as it is voiced) that will make sure he is not reversed. The first two are general: "I want to have a good life," and "I want to be miserable." The second two are specific. "I want to be able to go to sleep easily," and "I want to have trouble going to sleep." Test after each statement. If your subject tests strong after uttering negative statements and weak after uttering the positive statements, he is reversed. If that occurs, you must first treat for reversal.

When you know that the subject is not reversed, you can test the subject while he thinks about the feeling he has when he imagines himself falling asleep. Test for the phobia and then treat as indicated, usually by tapping the second toe of each foot as explained in chapter 7.

Anorexia and Bulimia

[These conditions require the attention of a professionally trained person who can supervise the treatment suggested here.]

Both *anorexia* and *bulimia* are eating disorders that are generally found in young women and girls ranging in age from 13 to 25. These two problems are very complex. *Anorexia,* where the patient simply stops eating, fear of being attractive as a sex object, and fear of growing up and facing adult responsibilities. *Bulimia,* where the patient overeats and then induces vomiting to keep from digesting the food, includes fear of starving, fear of hunger, as well as fear of being attractive as a sex object.

Some of thes unrealistic fears can be dealt with through the "Five-Minute" treatment. As with the problem of insomnia, a series of questions will be needed to determine just what fears are operating in any specific case.

Begin, as always, with the "clear" test and with a test for reversal. Then identify one fear by having the subject think about it (for example, imagine being overweight). Treat that fear. [Note: An excessive unrealistic fear of getting fat does not appear to help people to stay thin.]

When the subject tests strong on the fear of being fat you can go on to another fear. The same sort of questioning and testing can be used for bulimia, except now the questions will deal with the inability to stop eating, which is indicative of that affliction.

There are usually associated fears dwelling with need for love and acceptance in anorexia and bulimia, some of them deeply hidden. Statements dealing with self-acceptance must be included. An anorexic usually does not feel good about herself, nor does someone suffering from bulimia.

I advise anyone who suffers from any compound phobias or from physical-mental disturbances like anorexia and bulimia to see a qualified professional for more in-depth treatment. *Anorexia*, especially, can be a life-threatening condition, far too serious to be tampered with by an amateur. A need for self-acceptance, for example, which is a problem faced by both anorexic and bulimics, can be boosted by the use of the phrase "I profoundly and deeply accept myself." which we discussed before, but there may be many complications for the initial self-rejection that may not respond to this simple treatment.

Many approaches may be needed to help an anorexic or a bulimic to feel good about herself. She will have established many behavioral patterns that will need to be changed. She may need help in dressing, in applying makeup, in hair styling. She may need exercise that will build her body. However, I have found that eliminating basic fears by the use of the

"Five-Minute" treatment will make all the other steps toward health easier.

There are problems which people face that are so complicated they seem to defy treatment. Yet despite their involved complications, and considering my warnings regarding the need for specialized treatment in certain cases such as anorexia and dyslexia, there *is* a place for my "Five-Minute" treatment, even in these extreme cases. In fact, one of the most effective areas for use of the "Five-Minute" treatment may be in conjunction with other forms of therapy. For if the inhibiting fears can be eliminated, the way for treatment of possible underlying physical disorders is made clear.

Uncovering Subconscious Phobias

When a phobia is intense and severe, a phobic really *knows* it exists. But many people do not experience their phobias with any great force.They may have mild phobias which,though they restrict freedom of action in life, are not recognizable for what they truly are. A person having such mild phobias, however, may feel mind and body stresses of which he is not fully aware, since they generally become a "part of his existence." Yet, these stresses may harm him, and may inhibit his activities in ways he barely acknowledges.

I have seen a few sub-conscious phobias erupt into panic attacks, totally surpising the victim. Once such "explosion" took place when I asked a patient, a calm, thirty-five-year-old woman who was afraid of flying, if she had any other fears.

I posed the question to her because she had come to me for treatment of her fear of flying, and since she was not intending to travel by air for some months, I wanted to demonstrate the effectiveness of my treatment to her. I could not have her think about flying after the treatment to let her see that she was improved, because, even *before* the treatment, she had not been upset just by *thinking* of being in the air.

I asked her if she would be afraid to be in a small closet with the door closed. She answered that this would not bother her, and so I proceeded to use the arm test on her, while she *thought* about being in a closed closet.

She tested weak. Then I had her touch her stomach and again think of being in the closed closet. Now her arm was strong — suggesting that she actually had a phobia about such confinement.

She was surprised at the result and questioned its veracity. So I suggested that we go to a small closet in the room ajoining my office. She followed me bravely, but as she got closer to the closet she became more tentative and frightened. She stepped inside — and realized that she could not allow me to close the door.

I was pleased. This experience gave me a definite phobia with which to work so that she could see immediately if my "Five-Minute" treatment worked for her. (About 10 to 15% of the population are not responsive *at this printing* to the treatment.) I knew that with such proof, she would be more confident that, after my treatment for her flying fear, she would be free of it when she again had to fly.

Returning with her to my office, I proceeded with the "Five-Minute" treatment for her heretofore hidden fear. As soon as the treatment was complete, we returned to the closet, and now she entered it and closed the door. She told me she felt perfectly comfortable.

The argument could be made that since she was not aware of the fear it did no harm, and since in normal life one seldom shuts oneself into closets, nothing was gained by ridding her of this phobia. However, beyond the fact that it convinced her of the effectiveness of my "Five-Minute" treatment, this cure of a hidden fear did have other results. It relieved her body of a tension of which she had not been aware, since she had carried it so long.

I find that men, especially, seem to have more subconscious phobias than do women. Men also are more apt to deny the existence of phobias. Probably this tendency in men comes from our social conditioning. Men are taught that "only sissies are afraid." They tell themselves that they are not sissies, and therefore they cannot be afraid. This results in either a denial of a phobia or, at least, denying any *awareness* of the phobia.

This rejection of the possibility that a phobic exists does not help a person avoid the effects of the affliction. Many men, for example, who would never admit to being afraid of flying, still "tank up" with alcohol before any flight. It is easy to see that such an refusal to recognize a phobia does nothing to stop it from harming its victim. So hidden phobias do need to be identifed and eliminated, not by "smothering them" in alcohol or medication, but by effective treatment that will free their victims forever.

Test For Hidden Fears

If you are interested in determining whether or not you suffer from any hidden fears, study the following checklist. You might have a friend test you on any items that seem interesting. If your arm goes down when you think of any of the following, but strengthens when you touch one of the test spots (stomach or side, see Figures F & G) it is likely that you have a phobia.

☐ Answering machines
☐ Asking for a raise
☐ Asking for directions from strangers
☐ Asserting yourself
☐ Banking
☐ Bees
☐ Being late
☐ Being on time
☐ Being sexy
☐ Competitive situations
☐ Computers
☐ Complaining about unsatisfactory products or service
☐ Court appearance
☐ Crowds
☐ Dancing
☐ Dealing with a waiter
☐ Dentists
☐ Dining alone
☐ Falling in love
☐ Flying in bumpy weather
☐ Freeway, highway driving
☐ Frigidity
☐ Greeting other guests at a party or dinner
☐ Handling small creatures (pet mice or rats) and insects
☐ Heavy traffic
☐ Heights
☐ Hospitals
☐ Impotence
☐ Inquiring about promotional possibilities
☐ Looking around at people

☐ Needles & shots
☐ New job
☐ Nightmares
☐ Not being liked by everyone
☐ Panic
☐ Paying a check
☐ Physicians
☐ Pointed instruments
☐ Public speaking
☐ Saying no to a high pressure salesman
☐ Seasickness
☐ Seeking a job
☐ Sending back unacceptable dishes in a restaurant
☐ Social situations
☐ Snakes
☐ Speaking to an answering machine
☐ Spiders
☐ Starting new business
☐ Surgery
☐ Swallowing
☐ Talking to strangers
☐ Telephoning
☐ Telling jokes
☐ Telling someone you're too busy to talk when they phone at an inappropriate time.
☐ Tennis serve
☐ Tennis with people watching

You may want to add to the above list anything you would "prefer not to do," "could do without." or "would rather avoid."

You may find it interesting to use the arm test on every one of these fears and on any others you can think of. It may surprise you that hidden fears exist in you. A woman who discovered she had a phobia about talking to an answering machines was very surprised. She had known for years that she didn't like leaving messages, but she had not thought that she had a phobia. Once she treated herself, she found she was able to enjoy leaving messages to her friends, as far as she knew, for the first time in her life.

Troubleshooting

I have found that most laypeople who decide to try this cure, either for themselves or for a friend, are hesitant to act. They aren't accustomed to assuming the role of "healer" in any situation. Even a headache is generally treated with medicine prescribed by a physician. As a result, they tend to be uncertain in what they do.

It is important to understand that this hesitancy does not appear to have any effect on the cure. This is, in fact, one further demonstration that the "Five-Minute" treatment is not based on placebo effect, hypnotism or on the charisma of the operator. What is critical is that the tapping be done on the right spot, and that it be performed for a long enough time.

A Note About Phobias

Many times, an individual will have more than one phobia, and the fears will be clustered. In some of these situations, it may be helpful to identify each fear individually and treat each one separately. It is also important to remember what was said regarding psychological reversal in Chapter 5.

If the treatment does not seem to work, do not get immediately discouraged. Test again for recurring reversal, and correct that, for this is the usual cause of the problem. Then perform the treatment again. Now it will most probably work.

The Presence of Many Phobias

If you still are not successful, examine the subject for additional phobias and fears that might be inhibiting cure. Deal with each one individually, starting with the lesser fears and working up to the larger ones. There is also the possibility that a subconscious fear is at the root of the problem. Refer to Chapter 10, Uncovering Subconscious Fears. If it can't be identified, simply tell your subject to "think of any remaining fears" he has, and then test and treat him.

Other Inhibitions To Effective Cure

If this seems not to work, one of two things can be wrong. Firstly, you may not be tapping in the right place. Check again, to be sure you are doing it right. Secondly, the obstacle to cure may arise from recurring psychological reversal, perhaps brought on by unacknowledged conflict between you and the subject, if that is possible, or perhaps from some other cause. In any case, identify and treat.

A man of 62, married, recently fell in love with a woman in her twenties, but did not realize the depth of his involvement with her until she took a protracted vacation. Because he felt guilty about this involvement with the girl (he was already married), he had urged his mistress to have an affair during her trip through Europe — and she took him at his word.

However, he learned of her affair — which lasted throughout the journey — he was devastated. He had never experienced such pain before, since his courtship of his wife had been free of such conflicts. He was terrified that if his mistress didn't return to him, he would "grow old" and never enjoy sex again.

His wife knew of his affair. She was convinced that he would learn so much from the experience that he would return to her on an emotional level higher than they had ever shared before, so she wanted to help him through this problem. She brought her husband to me for treatment for the fear he had of losing his sexual vitality. He improved immediately.

I followed up the treatment by showing his wife how to reinforce the treatment if he needed that done. This man had been reversed before I treated him, and I knew he would probably snap back into reversal again, and with the reversal some of the fear would return.

This did occur, as I expected. But when his wife tried to treat him, she failed. She tried a number of times, each time beginning by attempting to correct the reversal, but she still was unsuccessful.

This was a situation where the husband's guilt interfered with the treatment offered by his wife. He could not accept help from her, since he was aware that he was hurting her very much by his actions. Her presence, because it stirred his guilt, kept putting him into reversal.

This emphasized something I had observed before. Often a married couple, or two people living together, can establish certain emotional relationships between them that interfere with the application of the "Five-Minute" treatment. They also can definitely affect each others moods and attitudes. One partner who is severely reversed can cause the other to experience reversal. It is possible for psychological reversal to affect every aspect of living. And, in its extreme form, it can be very difficult to handle. In cases where couples contribute to each others psychological reversal, repeated intensive treatment for the reversal for both is strongly recommended.

Psychological Reversal and Strong Negativism

I call the most severe complication of psychological reversal *Negative Psychological Infrastructure*. When an individual has this problem, it can present difficulties with which a layperson, attempting to free a relative or a friend of simple phobias, cannot cope.

Negative Psychological Infrastructure is that condition in which an individual responds negatively to *all* suggestions. We all know someone like that, and most of us, even on a social level, find it difficult to deal with such a person. In addition to *and complicating* the psychological reversal is the presence of an elaborate network of powerful negative habits of thinking.

In psychotherapy, this condition presents very definite problems, many of which have, in the past taken months —and often years — to overcome. I have found that this condition takes a combination of my "Five-Minute" treatment and a considerable amount of attitudinal re-education. It is not responsive to either one alone. So if, in your attempt to help yourself or a friend, you encounter this type of strong, generalized resistance, I advise that you turn the treatment over to a qualified psychotherapist who can deal with it on many levels.

When There Are Physical Problems

As I mentioned early in the book, the "Five-Minute" treatment serves to "repair" energy disruptions, allowing energy to flow freely through the problem meridian. But some people are biologically disposed toward energy disruptions. If an individual is hypoglycemic, for example, he may be more susceptible to phobias than is the average, normally healthy person. Some rare cases who don't respond to the "Five-Minute" treatment might need to be treated for hypoglycemia before he could be successfully freed of phobias. However, it is so easy to try the "Five-Minute" treatment, that there isn't much to lose. If a subject seems to be in reversal and resists treatment, a qualified orthomolecular practioner is indicated.*

Beliefs That Cause Resistance To Cure

Some people seem to cherish their phobias. They may even believe that they are better for having such problems. A few of these beliefs are discussed below, for they do interfere with any attempt to effect a cure.

*Orthomolecular Medical Society, 6151 W. Century Blvd., Los Angeles, CA 90045; Academy of Orthomolecular Psychiatry, 1691 Northern Blvd., Manhasset, NY 11031.

Fallacy #1 Symptom Substitution

I mentioned earlier Freud's theory that phobias were actually "safe" institutions for a deep-seated Oedipus Complex. It was a theory that Freud taught and used as a basis for his theory. According to him and to his orthodox followers, a patient who suffers from a severe phobia or who is a victim of compulsive behavior is actually "masking" his sexual desire for his mother (and a compensating wish to see his father dead) with this seemingly unrelated mental problem. His conclusion was that if the therapist could help the patient overcome this "Oedipus Complex" he would cure the phobia.

When I was teaching psychology in the sixties, I, along with most of my colleagues, was guilty of perpetuating this theory, which was called "symptom substitution." Part and parcel of this theory was the belief that were the psychologist to remove the phobia without tackling the underlying oedipal complex, another phobia would "rush in" to fill the void.

The principal seemed reasonable. If, in fact, phobias were "masking devices," then if one mask were removed, another would be needed — immediately.

The problem was that no part of the theory worked. Psychotherapy took years, and it resulted in the exposing of many inner conflicts. Sometimes the therapist was even able to "root out" some deep, hidden hatred for a parent. But no matter what the therapist did, he seldom actually cured his patient. The orthodox Freudian theory was abandoned by many, at last, *because it did not work.*

The difficulty is that general understanding of changes in psychological theories lags far behind the advanced thinkers in the field. As a result, many laypeople still believe that psychotherapy for phobias requires years of treatment and that, if the therapist is "foolish" enough to eliminate a symptom instead of attacking the "underlying cause" of difficulty, his patient will simply have that symptom replaced by another which probably will be far more painful or disruptive.

Suffice it to say that just as the theory of "Oedipus Complex" being the basic problem was abandoned by forward-thinking psychologists, so was the belief that eliminating a fear would leave a vacuum which would be filled with another fear. Since the concept of Oedipal Substitution has been put in serious doubt simply because treatment based on it does not work, the "sister" theory (that a phobia is necessary to keep an individual from facing an unpleasant truth about himself) is also left without support. Over the last 20 years, many therapists from many differing schools of thought have been eliminating symptoms in their patients with only positive benefits.

When my client (mentioned earlier in the book) lost her fear of water after the "Five-Minute" treatment, no phobia of equal proportions took its place. She was simply freed of her fear of water. This was accompanied by a growing sense of well-being and noticeable improvement in general self-confidence.

Fallacy #2: Fears Create Character

An aggressive salesman was convinced that his success was caused by the manner in which he falsely pretended to himself that he had no fear of public speaking and new people. For a long time he refused to acknowledge that he had a problem. But finally he became so frightened as he stood facing a large number of potential clients that he was unable to give his presentation.

It was only then that he sought help.

But he still feared the effect on his personality of losing his phobia. Phobias, he insisted, were character forming. They gave people depth.

Fortunately, I was able to convince him that this belief was untrue. I presented many examples of patients who had possessed specific characteristics before they were treated and showed that those characteristics did not vanish just because the phobias that caused them so much pain were gone.

He decided to go ahead with treatment. He is still an aggressive salesman with an excellent record and substantial income. The difference is that now he is happier than he was before. When he lost his fear of talking in public, he lost none of his cleverness and excellent ability as a salesman.

Fallacy #3: Phobias Make People Creative

Creativity is an invaluable gift. So is artistic ability, the ability to deliver a song or act a role. No one can really explain why some people are creative, artistic, musical, inventive, and others are not. It is this nebulous characteristic of creativity that causes the problem. Since a creative person cannot explain the origin of his creativity, he dares not change any of the circumstances that surround it.

The resistance is even greater when emotional or mental changes are suggested. Phobias are cherished when their victims believe that they may be partially responsible for the presence of talent. *Phobias do only harm.*

I have practiced for years in the Los Angeles/Hollywood area, and before that in New York and Detroit, and I have treated many creative artists. One patient, a talented composer of background music for films, came to me because she had a very real dread of blank paper. Yet, she was reluctant to cooperate in seeking a "full cure." What she wanted was to have her fear brought under control. She insisted that the fear itself was what motivated her to fill the paper as soon as possible.

She did get rid of her phobia. But she was not particularly happy about it until she settled down once more and began to create a new score. When she realized that, if anything, her creativity flowed more easily than before, she returned to thank me for "what I had done." But she still expressed surprise that she did not need the phobia to be creative.

Fallacy #4: The Competitive Edge

Actors and athletes share a confusion that makes them both reluctant to seek help to rid themselves of phobias or deep-seated fears. The difficulty lies in their inability to differentiate between fear and excitement. Excitement "gears up" a person so that he is alert, ready to deal with any emergency. This is something an actor or athlete needs. Inspired by passion and excitement, he has an advantage over an equally skilled doctor or athlete who does not feel that thrill as he steps into the limelight.

Fear, on the contrary, serves to disrupt a performance, causing an actor to "blow his lines" or to deliver them weakly. It can interfere with an athlete's natural body flow, "tripping him up" just as he prepares to leap, throw, or hit a ball.

This same confusion regarding the conflicting effects of phobias and excitement sometimes causes a public speaker or a politician to hesitate to enter treatment. They need to understand that excitement gives passion to their words. Fear can trip them up and cause them to forget what they have to say.

If you are dealing with a subject who believes any of these fallacies, you will have to either convince him that they are wrong or find another subject.

Summary

What needs to be emphasized here is that this "Five-Minute" treatment in the hands of the layman can — and will — eliminate many painful phobias and fears that inhibit happy living. But it cannot cure everyone, nor is it a total substitute for therapy of a more conventional kind. It is, however, a tool that can give countless numbers freedom from fear for the first time in their lives.

One other point that is important. This "Five-Minute" treatment cannot harm the individual, even if it is blocked in effectiveness because of extreme psychological reversal. As such, it is unique among treatments for phobias and fears. Even in the hands of a layman, this cure can do no harm. And it can do great good.

Applications
And
Implications

Always, when a new method of dealing with old problems is discovered, the question arises as to how it can be applied to specific situations. Parents, teachers, students, business people, even children, can use the "Five-Minute" treatment for phobias and fears effectively.

Parents are often faced with the problem of dealing with childhood fears which, if left untended, could affect the child for years to come. Two young parents, Bob and May, brought their two-year old son to the shore of Lake Michigan on a particulary stormy day. Since they and their older son all enjoyed the strength of the waves, they did not think that the younger boy would be upset. However, he became frightened, and cried every time they carried him close to the surf. It is important to note that nothing drastic happened to frighten him. The fear was spontaneous.

At this point, the fear was not deep-seated. However, if it was not dealt with, it could develop further, and could become a severe handicap.

This young couple proceeded to go through a long series

of reconditioning steps with their son. First they bought him a small plastic pool, where the water was very controlled. He enjoyed playing in it. However, he seemed a bit frightened of being sprayed by the hose, so they kept the hose on the ground.

Gradually, over the summer, they helped him progess from still water to a narrow stream, where the water was flowing gently. They brought him to that stream often, gradually moving their play closer to the water's edge until, at last, the child was happily splashing his hands in the stream.

Now they picked a day when the lake was quiet and brought their son to the beach. He played happily by the shore, even venturing into the low surf. By this method they finally reached a point where, on a stormy day, they were able once more to bring their son to the lake. This time, he enjoyed the force of the storm and the power of the waves as much as did his older brother.

The fact was, however, that this reconditioning had taken all summer, and had consumed both parents' attention every time the family went on an outing. The "Five-Minute" treatment could have had the same effect in a matter of minutes.

When a child experiences fear in a given situation, parents deal with it immediately, while the fear still exists in its least formidable condition.

The treatment can be used to eliminate the fear a child feels during a nightmare. By simply tapping the second toes of the child while he is telling you about the dream, the fear will likely subside. The child will be able to go back to sleep without anyone spending a long time in the middle of the night trying to calm him down.

Teachers can use the treatment in much the same way as it is used by parents, since teachers often find themselves present when a child first experiences a phobic reaction. When a teacher is taking a classroom of children on a field trip, it is awkward and difficult for her to have to give special attention to a child who has fear of busses, or elevated trains, or any of the myriad situations to which the class may be exposed. The "Five-Minute" treatment can free the child of his terror and simplify the entire trip for both that child and for the teacher.

Students, especially older students who are coping with tests, oral presentations, and recitations which they fear, can at last overcome the fear through the use of the "Five-Minute" treatment.

Gladys, a good student, was faced with an exam in anatomy which she was sure she could not pass. She was besieged with visions of her upcoming failure. She saw the disappointment her mother would experience when she heard her daughter had not passed. She even visualized herself a "drop-out" from medical school because she had failed that particular exam.

Gladys used the "Five-Minute" treatment while thinking of these "pictures of failure." One by one, she eliminated her fears of failure until she was able to consider the exam without such terror. All in all, the process took her about fifteen minutes. Because she had studied, and did know the answers, she passed the exam with flying colors. But she realized, as anyone who has felt similar fear of failure will agree, that had she not overcome the fear, it might well have interfered so severely with the flow of ideas that she could have failed. ·

Business people, or performers are not safe from the inhibitions created by phobias and fear. We have read about fear of flying interfering with a commitment. But a fear as simple as that of talking on the telephone can cause great havoc in a career. This is the day of communication — and much what we say to business associates is necessarily said over the phone.

Arthur could not comfortably talk on the phone. When he had to carry on an extended conversation, his palms sweated, his heart raced, his pulse grew rapid. He was in severe discomfort throughout the call. As a result, he became abrupt and almost rude in his hurry to end his misery. However, he felt very foolish about his phobia, and so never explained why he was rude on the phone when in person he was a "nice guy," and easy to get along with.

This was more than a small annoyance for both Arthur and for his employer. Much of the company business was transacted over the phone, and Arthur's poor phone personality was a threat to the business — and to his job. He knew that if he could not change, he would be fired.

The "Five-Minute" treatment solved Arthur's problem. When he no longer was in a panic when talking on the phone, his true warm personality began to come through. Business associates whom he had never met in person, but with whom he had carried on a rocky relationship over the phone, noticed immediately that he had changed. He no longer had the problems that had always accompanied any telephone business he had to transact.

His job was no longer in jeopardy. In time, as business associates became accustomed to Arthur's new phone personality, they forgot how difficult working with him had been in the past. But Arthur did not forget. He knew that in a very real way his job effectiveness had been helped greatly by a short treatment which, when it was suggested to him, seemed too simple and easy to be true.

Children can use this "Five-Minute" treatment, too, since, it cannot harm them, even if they do not do it right, and if performed correctly, it can save them much distress. If a child is in a position where he has in the past experienced a phobic reaction which was treated by his parents, he might feel a little of that fear return when, alone, he first encounters the object or circumstance that arouses the fear.

Walter had experienced a spontaneous fear of automobiles when he was at an airport with his father and they tried to cross a busy roadway. His father had treated the fear with the "Five-Minute" treatment, and it had vanished. He had then shown Walter how to reinforce the treatment by tapping the bone just below his eye sockets while thinking of the fear.

Some weeks later, Walter was on a field trip at school. The children were in Garfield Park, in Chicago, and had to walk through a large parking lot to get to the door of the Natural History Museum. As he left his seat in the bus, Walter felt a recurrence (which rarely happens) of the fear that had almost immobilized him at the airport. Immediately, he tapped the bones below his eye sockets. He did not have to try to visualize the cause of his fear — he was experiencing it. The tapping was barely noticed by his fellow classmates. By the time it was Walter's turn to step out of the bus, he was calm again. His reinforcement had saved him from a terror-provoking experience.

Medical fears. In this world of technology, anyone facing medical care is also facing some specific test, which may easily become the object of a phobia. Some specific ones are fear of a liver scan test, fear of a CATscan, fear of needles, and fear of surgery.

The liver scan test usually provokes anxiety. It is not a routine test, and people who take it usually are suspected of having some serious medical condition. The anxiety they feel before taking the test is not allayed by the test itself. If the subject fears needles, he must first face a shot of radioactive material, which is put in the veins. This also provokes a fear of radioactivity and radiation exposure, even when the physician reassures his patient that there is no danger.

Now the patient must lie down while a huge monster machine hovers over him. A claustrophobic patient would be in terror from this alone. Many fears contend for the patient's attention. Certainly, this test could frighten any patient who was not properly prepared.

Similarly, the *CATscan* can trigger a claustrophobic patient. He must lie on a narrow platform beneath a behemoth of a machine through which he must slowly pass by way of a small circular hole. This is another situation that can rouse deep fears in any susceptible patient.

The fear of needles is better known, since we are given shots on many occasions. So, also is the generalized fear of surgery. Yet both can cause extreme pain to the patient if they are not considered before the shot or the surgery begins.

The "Five-Minute" treatment can be used by any physician, nurse, or assistant who wishes to help his patient through these difficult situations. A few seconds treating for claustrophobia before the CATscan will make the examination far less traumatic to the frightened patient. Shots will leave no psychological scars if they are administered *after* the "Five-Minute" treatment. Even the trauma of going in for a liver scan, with all its accompanying anxieties, will be eased if some of the major phobias and fears that the test arouses are first laid to rest through the "Five-Minute "treatment.

Every human situation has similar examples of where the "Five-Minute" treatment can be effective. What needs to be remembered is that in such "emergency" situations, the testing can be bypassed. The fear is generally obvious, and can be dealt with directly. This is particularly true if the testing has been done sometime prior to the emergency, so that the subject knows what is bothering him. Then he can treat himself for that particular fear of phobia.

The implication of this aspect of the "Five-Minute" treatment is exciting to anyone who has suffered from phobic reactions. The immediacy of the treatment, applied while the fear is strong, means cutting the time of terror short. It means that an individual can deal quickly and effectively with his own fear, without involving others in the process.

Most of all, it means that all those many situations that have, in the past, been ruined by unreasonable fears can be enjoyed. Even if the treament entailed some ridiculous form of behavior, most phobics would consider the rewards worth the few moments of feeling "silly." But in fact, since in a public situation the reinforcement of treatment (or the treatment itself) can be confined to tapping the bone under the eye sockets, it can be performed without arousing undue attention. Most people would merely assume that the action was a nervous behaviorism and ignore it. But to the phobic who, by this simple act, relieved himself of an overpowering fear, the act would be like opening the gates of a prison before they had succeeded in slamming closed for the rest of his life. In the future you will probably see people all over the place doing this.

Living
Without
Fear

For the phobic sufferer, the very title of this chapter seems unreal. Yet, certainly if we are entitled to the "pursuit of happiness," which our Constitution guarantees us, we must be able to live our lives without fear. For fear destroys happiness.

We are encouraged, as we develop, to consider life-limiting conditions as not only acceptable, but sometimes as essential. Our religious or moral instruction puts limits on behavior, restricting us and denying us experiences that could contribute to our growth. Yet we do not rebel against such limitations. We consider them essential for our "greater good." Certainly for anyone who sincerely believes in the tenets of their religion, those restrictions are important, and should not be violated.

However, there are many restrictions that we place on ourselves because we do not know how to deal with unreasonable fears and phobias. These restrictions are limiting to our spiritual happiness, and should not be endured.

Returning for a moment to the first woman I treated with

my "Five-Minute" treatment for phobias. I had been aware, during the year and a half when I treated her by conventional methods, of how painful her fear of water was to her. Her mother, discussing her problem, was able to clarify how restricting this fear had been — and how long it had existed.

There was, her mother explained, no time when she could remember when her daughter was not terrified of water. It had kept her from swimming classes in high school, had interfered with her fun at picnics, had made a trip to amusement parks impossible, since water plays a large part in not only the decor but in the rides available in both places.

As she grew, the fear of water influenced where she went to school, where she worked, what forms of recreation she could enjoy. She had never had an opportunity to appreciate the beauty of Big Sur, or the glory of a sunset over the ocean, because her fear of water precluded her going to such locations. She even had trouble visiting friends who had pools, for if they had a party in their back yard and she had to be near a pool, she was in trouble. She could not join the other guests in the yard.

Once the fear of water was removed, all these things changed. Suddenly she was free not only to enjoy the beauty of the sunset over the ocean and the power of a storm, she was free also to travel to places that had heretofore been inaccessible to her. She was, in a very real way, released from a prison whose walls were defined by her phobia.

This is true of all phobics. When they finally are released from their fears, they find a new world available to them. They can fly, talk over the phone, walk through malls and shop in fascinating little out-of-the-way stores. They can smell flowers and feel rain on their cheeks. They can revel in all the wonders this world has to offer — wonders that they had believed were never to be part of their experience.

This, then, is what the "Five-Minute" treatment can give to the phobic sufferer. Immediate freedom — immediate liberation from the shackles fear has put upon them for so long.

A person who has never experienced a phobic fear can't quite understand how dramatic this release can be. The most graphic photograph of a prisoner stepping out into the world after years of confinement behind prison walls cannot fully illustrate this emotional release. For the freed phobic is released from inner bars that held in his spirit. And in this new freedom, he regains his happiness, his optimism, his joy in living. It is, certainly, an experience no phobic should be denied.

* * *

For information on audio and video cassettes and on Dr. Callahan's Workshops, write to Dr. Roger Callahan, P.O. Box 11082, Marina Del Rey, CA 90295.

* * *

To enter your name on our mailing list and receive further phobia treatment information as it becomes available, send your name and address to: Enterprise Publishing, Inc., 725 Market Street, Wilmington, DE 19801.

Summary
Workbook

The instructions for using the "Five-Minute" treatment are in Chapters 7 & 8. However, if you need only a quick review of the process, this workbook section will provide the needed information. We all have experienced a need for a refresher course, even after we have mastered some technique. So in this workbook you will find not only a summary of the "Five-Minute" treatment itself, but also of the method of testing and the treatment for psychological reversal.

Testing

1) Two people are needed for testing.

2) Before testing, tester should determine that there is no reason (medical, athletic strain, injury, etc.) why pressure should not be put on the arm.

3) Tester and subject should stand facing each other.

4) If tester is right-handed, subject extends left arm straight out from the shoulder with palm down. Reverse this if the tester is left handed.

5) Tester places left hand on subjects shoulder and right hand open on the wrist of subject's extended arm.

6) First test is for "clear" reaction. Pressure (approximately 15 pounds — press on bathroom scale to "feel" what 15 pounds of pressure is) is put on arm to identify point of resistance. This will be identifiable by noting how the arm seems to "lock" against pressure. The amount of pressure needed to feel this "locking" is all that will be needed during the test. Ask subject to resist this pressure.

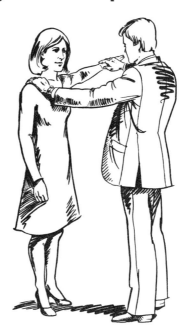

Figure A
Test Position

7) Second test will be to identify the difference between reaction of muscles to a true statement and a false one. Have subject state his correct name, and test his arm. It should test strong. Now have him state a false name. His arm should test weak. These two tests will give you a "feel" for this particular subject's strength and responses.

Testing for psychological reversal

As a general precaution, the subject should be tested for psychological reversal before any test for phobias is given. This will allow the tester to prepare to deal with the reversal and so avoid the discouragement of having the treatment fail the first time it is performed.

1) Using the arm position described above, the tester has the subject made two statements, testing after each one.

2) The first statement is "I want to get over my fear of ... [here the name of the object or circumstance feared should be given]. The arm should be tested. If it is weak, the next statement should also be tested.

3) The subject now repeats "I want to keep my fear of ..." The arm is tested again. If it tests strong now, the subject is psychologically reversed. the subject cannot be treated successfully until the psychological reversal is corrected.

4) If the subject tests strong on *both* statements, then the *tester and the subject are both reversed.* This condition must be dealt with (using the treatment described below) before treatment can continue.

Psychological Reversal Treatment

In the following procedures, the speaking and tapping should be performed simultaneously.

1) The subject repeats three times the self-affirming statement — with conviction: "Even though I have this fear, I

profoundly and deeply accept myself."

    2) The subject vigorously taps the outside of either hand with the fingers of the other hand 35 times. (See Figure D.)

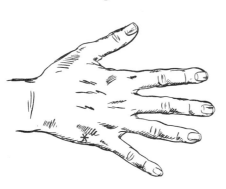

Figure D
Reversal Treatment Spot

Figure E
Reversal Treatment

    3) Repeat procedure with other hand.

    This procedure should correct reversal, if not permanently, at least for a long enough time to permit effective treatment and cure of the phobia. If the subject is *not* reversed and treatment is done, it will simply have no effect.

Testing For Phobias and Fears

    1) The subject thinks of his fear or phobia while the tester performs the arm-muscle test. The muscle should test weak. If it does not, again check for psychological reversal.

2) Now the subject places his right fingers on his stomach (approximately 3 inches above navel) and again thinks about the object or situation which he fears. Usually, the arm will then test strong. This will indicate that the phobia or fear is connected to an imbalance of the stomach meridian.

(Note: If the arm tests weak on the stomach area, it means that the phobia isn't connected to the stomach area. Touch the phobia test spot #2 (to the side of the body on the last rib — either right or left depending on whether tester is right- or left-handed) and use the arm test again. If the arm now tests strong, proceed with the treatment, using treatment spot #2. This search will usually not be necessary, since the greatest majority of phobias are connected to the phobia test spot #1.)

The Treatment

Any one of the following treatments is effective, though the first listed is preferred because there is no chance of injury during performance of the therapy. During all treatments the subject must be thinking of his/her phobia.

Treatment For Test Spot 1:

1) With the tip of the index finger, tap the subject's second toe (next to the big toe) 35 times below the nail and slightly on the side furthest from the big toe. This should be performed on both feet.

Figure I
Treatment Point for
Test Point #1

2) With the tips of the index finger and the middle finger, tap the edge of the bone of the eye socket just beneath and centered on the bone under the eye for about 30 seconds or 35 times. This should be done on both sides of the face. Note: This tapping should be gentler than in #1, in order to avoid injury.

Figure J
Treatment Point for
Test Point #1

Treatment For Test Spot 2:

1) Same as treatment for test spot 1, only tap outside of big toe.

2) Same as treatment for test spot 1, only tap both sides of the body on the fifth rib up from the lowest rib.

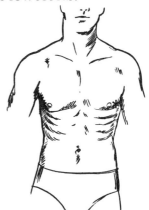

Figure I.a
Treatment Point for
Test Point #2

Figure H
Treatment Points for
Test Point #2

Eye Closure And Eye Open Test And Treatment

1) Test subject with eyes closed. If arm goes weak, tap back of both of his hands (one at a time) between the pinky and the ring finger while his eyes are closed.

2) Test subject with eyes open and repeat same procedure as with eyes closed.

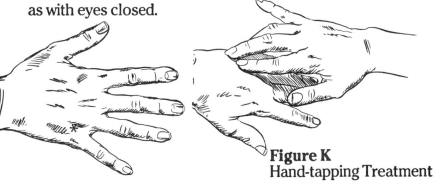

Figure K
Hand-tapping Treatment

Additional Treatments For Test Spots 1 & 2

1) Have subject hum a simple tune (Yankee Doodle Dandy) while you tap the back of both hands vigorously 35 times. (See Figure K.)

2) Repeat hand tapping as above, except have subject recite multiplication tables aloud instead of humming.

3) Have subject put eyes in a down left position and tap back of both hands as above. Repeat with eyes in a down right position.

Figure L
Eye Position — down left

Figure M
Eye Position — down right

4) Have subject roll eyes to the left (counter-clockwise) illustrated below and tap back of hands as above. Repeat with subject rolling eyes to the right (clockwise).

Figure N
Eye Roll — to the left
(counter-clockwise)

Figure O
Eye Roll — to the right
(clockwise)

Verification

It is desirable that the patient experience the change that has occurred as a result of the treatment as soon as possible. This verification may be easy (as in the case of the girl in the observation tower or the woman who feared water), or it may be impossible. If verification cannot be accomplished immediately following cure, be sure to instruct the subject in the tapping procedure, so he can reinforce the cure just before he finds himself in a situation that in the past brought his phobia into play.

Note: If the subject is found to be reversed at the time of treatment, instruct him on how to test for and correct reversal (Chapter 5), so he can do that before reinforcing the treatment, if it becomes necessary.

Treating Yourself

1) (Assuming test spot 1, since testing cannot be done by yourself.) Think of phobia and tap 35 times under each eye. Supplement this by tapping second toes 35 times.

2) If fear persists, treat for test spot 2 by tapping 35 times on both sides of the body on the fifth rib up from lowest rib. Supplement by tapping 35 times on outside of each big toe.

3) If the fear persists, continue with additional conditions and treatments. Perform the following one at a time. After each treatment, if the fear persists, move on to the next treatment.

— Keep your eyes closed and tap the back of each hand (between pinky and ring finger) 35 times.

— Keep your eyes open and tap the back of each hand 35 times.

— Hum a simple tune (Yankee Doodle Dandy) and tap the back of each hand 35 times.

— Recite multiplication tables and tap the back of each hand 35 times.

— Look down and to the left and tap the back of each hand 35 times.

— Look down and to the right and tap the back of each hand 35 times.

— Roll your eyes to the left (counter-clockwise) and tap the back of each hand 35 times.

— Roll your eyes to the right (clockwise) and tap the back of each hand 35 times.

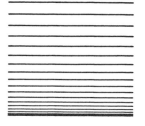

Phobia
Dictionary

Fear of:	Scientific Name
Albumin in the urine	Albuminrophobia
Anemia	Anemophobia
Animals	Zoophobia
Bacteria	Bacteriophobia
Beards	Pagonophobia
Beating	Mastigophobia
Bees	Apiphobia
Being alone	Autophobia, Monophobia, or Ermitophobia
Birds	Ornithophobia
Blood	Hemaphobia or Hemophobia
Blushing	Erythrophobia
Body odor	Bromidrosiphobia
Bullets	Ballistophobia
Bulls	Taurophobia
Cancer	Cancerphobia, Cancerophobia, or Carcinophobia
Cats	Ailurophobia
Childbirth	Tocophobia

Fear of:	Scientific Name
Children	Pedophobia
Chinese	Sinophobia
Cholera	Cholerophobia
Churches	Ecclesiophobia
Clouds	Nephophobia
Coitus	Coitophobia
Cold	Cheimaphobia or Cheimatophobia
Color	Chromophobia
Comets	Cometophobia
Computers	Computerophobia or Compuphobia
Confinement	Claustrophobia
Constipation	Coprostasophobia
Corpses	Necrophobia
Crossing a bridge	Gephyrophobia
Crossing a street	Agyrophobia
Crowds	Agoraphobia
Crystals	Crystallophobia
Dampness	Hygrophobia
Darkness	Achluophobia or Scotophobia
Dawn	Eosophobia
Death	Thanatophobia
Demons	Demonphobia
Depth	Bathophobia
Diabetes	Diabetophobia
Dirt	Mysophobia
Disease	Nephophobia or Pathophobia
Dogs	Cynophobia
Double vision	Diplopiaphobia
Draft	Aerophobia
Drink	Potophobia

Fear of:	Scientific Name
Drugs	Pharmacophobia
Dust	Koniophobia or Amathophobia
Electricity	Electrophobia
Enclosed places	Claustrophobia
English	Anglophobia
Everything	Panphobia or Pantophobia
Eyes	Ommetaphobia
Failure	Kakorraphiaphobia
Falling in love	Amorophobia
Fatigue	Kopophobia
Feathers	Pteronophobia
Fear	Phobophobia
Feces	Coprophobia
Fever	Febriphobia
Fire	Pyrophobia
Fish	Ichthyophobia
Floods	Antlophobia
Flowers	Anthophobia
Flutes	Aulophobia
Fog	Homichlophobia
Food	Cibophobia, Sitophobia, or Sitiophobia
Foreigners	Xenophobia
Freedom	Eleutherophobia
French	Francophobia or Gallophobia
Flying	Aerophobia
Fur	Doraphobia
Germans	Germanophobia or Teutonophobia
Germs	Spermophobia or spermatophobia
Ghosts	Plasmophobia
God	Theophobia

Fear of:	Scientific Name
Going to bed	Clinophobia
Gold	Aurophobia
Gravity	Barophobia
Gringos	Gringophobia
Hair	Chaetophobia or Trichophobia
Hair disease	Trichopathophobia
Heart disease	Cardiophobia
Heat	Thermophobia
Heaven	Uranophobia or Ouranophobia
Hell	Hadephobia or Stygiophobia
Heredity	Patriophobia
High places	Acrophobia, Altophobia, Bathophobia, or Hypsophobia
Home	Ecophobia, Oecophobia, or Oikophobia
Horses	Hippophobia
Ice or Frost	Cryophobia
Ideas	Ideophobia
Idleness	Thaasophobia
Imperfection	Atelophobia
Infinity	Apeirophobia
Innoculation	Trypanophobia or Vaccinophobia
Insanity	Lyssophobia or Maniaphobia
Insects	Entomophobia
Itching	Acarophobia
Japanese	Japanophobia
Jealousy	Zelophobia
Jews	Judeophobia
Justice	Dikephobie
Lakes	Limnophobia
Lice	Pediculophobia

Fear of:	Scientific Name
Light	Photophobia
Light flashes	Selaphobia
Lightning	Astraphobia
Magic	Rhabdophobia
Marriage	Gametophobia
Men	Androphobia
Meningitis	Meningitophobia
Metal	Metallophobia
Mice	Musophobia
Microbes	Bacillophobia or Microbiophobia
Mirrors	Eisoptrophobia
Mites	Acarophobia
Mobs	Ochlophobia
Money	Chrometophobia
Monsters	Teratophobia
Motion	Dromophobia or Kinetophobia
Music	Musicophobia
Names	Onomatophibia
Narrowness	Anginophobia
Needles	Belonephobia
Negroes	Negrophobia
New things	Neophobia
Night	Nyctophobia
Nudity	Gymnophobia or Nudophobia
One of anything	Monophobia
Open places	Agoraphobia
Pain	Algophobia
Parasites	Parasitophobia
Passage of time	Chronophobia
Passing high buildings	Batophobia

Fear of:	Scientific Name
Pellagra	Pellagraphobia
People	Anthropophobia
Philosophy	Philosophobia
Pins	Enetophobia
Pleasure	Hedonophobia
Poison	Toxiphobia, Tocophobia, or Tocicophobia
Politics	Politicophobia
Pope	Papaphobia
Poverty	Peniaphobia
Precipices	Cremnophobia
Priests	Hierophobia
Protein	Proteinphobia
Punishment	Poinephobia
Rabies	Hydrophobiophobia
Rectum	Rectophobia
Reptiles	Bactrachophobia or Herpetophobia
Responsibility	Hypegiaphobia
Ridicule	Katagelophobia
Rivers	Potamophobia
Robbers	Harpaxophobia
Ruin	Atephobia
Russians	Russophobia
Satan	Satanophobia
Scabies	Scabiophobia
Sea	Thalassophobia
Sex	Erotophobia or Genophobia
Shadows	Sciophobia
Sharpness	Acrophobia
Shock	Hormephobia
Sin	Hamartophobia or Pecatiphobia

Fear of:	Scientific Name
Skin	Dermatosiophobia
Skin disease	Dermatopathophobia
Sleep	Hypnophobia
Slime	Blennophobia or Myxophobia
Small things	Microphobia
Smell	Olfactophobia, Osmophobia, or Ophresiophobia
Smothering	Pnigophobia or Pnigerophobia
Snakes	Ophiciophobia, Ophiophobia, or Snakephobia
Snow	Chionophobia
Soiling	Rypophobia
Sound	Acousticophobia
Sourness	Acerophobia or Acerbophobia
Specific places	Topophobia
Speech	Lalophobia, Laliophobia, Glassophobia, or Phonophobia
Speed	Tachophobia
Spiders	Arachnephobia
Spirits	Penumatophobia
Standing	Stasophobia
Stars	Siderophobia
Stealing	Kleptophobia
String	Linonophobia
Sun	Heliophobia
Swallowing	Phagophobia
Symmetry	Symmetrophobia
Syphilis	Syphilophobia
Taste	Geumatophobia
Teeth	Odontophobia
Telephone	Telephonophobia
Thinking	Phronemophobia

Fear of:	Scientific Name
Thirteen	Tredecaphobia or Triskaidekaphobia
Thunder	Brontophobia, Tonitorophobia, or Keraunophobia
Touch	Haptophobia, Haphophobia, or Thixophobia
Travel	Hodophobia
Trembling	Tremophobia
Trichinosis	Trichinophobia
Tuberculosis	Tuberculophobia or Phthisiophobia
Tyrants	Tyrannophobia
Urine	Urophobia
Vehicles	Ochophobia
Venereal disease	Venereophobia
Void	Kenophobia
Vomiting	Emetophobia
Water	Hydrophobia or Aquaphobia
Waves	Cymophobia
Weakness	Asthenophobia
Wind	Anchraophobia
Women	Gynephobia
Words	Logophobia
Work	Ergophobia
Worms	Vermiphobia or Helminthophobia
Wound, injury	Traumatophobia
Writing	Graphophobia
Young girls	Parthenophobia

Statements
From
Treatment
Users

Fear of Dogs

"Between the ages of two and three, I witnessed a dog fight in which one dog bit the throat out of the other. This was imprinted so vividly in my mind, every detail remains as clear today as it was 48 years ago. As a result, all of my life I have had a great fear of all dogs — friendly or otherwise. I would get bumps on my skin, the hair on my neck would rise and I would experience an overall uncomfortable feeling to the point of panic.

Worst of all have been the recurring nightmares at the rate of two or three a month. As a child I did not understand them, but as I got older the reasons for them grew clear to me. I learned that many things could trigger them. Just seeing a wolf or a vicious dog on television; being in close contact with a dog, no matter how friendly, could incite one. The nightmare was always the same. I would be standing on the ground when a black dog would charge, lunging at my throat. I couldn't move. It was so real, I could smell his odor and could feel his hot breath on me. I would awaken screaming and would feel the same uncomfortable feeling of fear that I experience when I see a real dog.

After the treatment I must admit that I was skeptical and did not really expect anything to change. However, a few days later I was put to the test. About a block from my home live some people with a pit bulldog. I know this dog to be friendly, yet in years past, even as I would drive by in my auto and would see the dog out in the yard, the fear would be overwhelming. I would know that he couldn't harm me while in the safety of my car, yet the fear would still persist. On this particular day, however, the dog was in the yard and as I drove by I experienced no fear whatsoever. I pulled my car over, got out, walked across the street, walked past the house, and the dog lay there, maybe ten or fifteen feet away. He looked at me and I felt no fear. It was incredible that after 48 years I could bring myself to do this.

It has been three months, I have had no nightmares, and there is no question in my mind that my fear of dogs is completely gone. I am grateful for the treatment as it can be a mini-hell to go through life with a fear as great as the one I lived with all those years."

Robert Killner
Anaheim, CA

Fear of Flying

"We made it home finally. It was a long journey and I did really well on the plane ride home. It was almost 10 hours and a good flight. I was not nervous at all and slept most of the way. I would not have any qualms about flying to Los Angeles again someday. I no longer feel scared or nervous when I think about flying. In fact I enjoyed the flight back.

Thank you again so much for your help. If you are ever in Scotland be sure to look us up. All the best to you."

Vicki Blair
Perthshire, Scotland

Fear of Water

"For as long as I or my parents can remember I had been deeply troubled by a terrible fear of water. I could never go near water, whether it was a lake, pond, swimming pool or ocean. I couldn't even look at pictures of water or television without getting sick to my stomach. I was terrified by rain storms, afraid that it would flood and take me away. It is no exaggeration to say that I was more afraid of water than I was of death.

I had received psychological treatment for this fear for a year and a half and it resulted in just the slightest decrease in my fear. I still wouldn't leave the house if it rained and I still got ill to my stomach and a headache if I looked at water. The nightmares about water were still there also as they had been since I was a child.

I received treatment for this problem by Dr. Callahan and I was completely cured in a matter of minutes. I knew right away that I was finally over this horrible fear. I went right out to a swimming pool and looked the water right in the eye and for the first time in my life it dodn't bother me.

That night there was a terrible storm with wind and rain. I drove to the ocean to test out myself and I felt wonderful. I stood at the shore in the rain and the wind and I felt just fine.

Since that day I have not had a single nightmare about water.

That was five and a half years ago. I am 52 years old now.

Three years ago I saw Dr. Callahan again about a fear of standing up and talking in public. I would never do that and my church asked me to take a leading role in the activities which required me to address the whole congregation. I was terrified but I asked Dr. Callahan if he though he could help me with that and he said "Let's find out." Ever since he used his "Five-Minute" cure on me I have been enjoying getting up and talking in front of the whole church. It is now fun instead of terror!"

Mary Ford
Los Angeles, CA

Always Being Late

"I cannot express how much less hectic my life is since your cure of my phobia of never being "on time." I can rarely in my life remember arriving for anything "on time," or early. I used to try very hard to trick myself into departing *early* so as to arrive in a timely manner. I would most often feel anxious, and even panic, if it was an important appointment (i.e., an interview or catching an airplane). Now, however, I amazingly seem to be arriving *on time* without consciously thinking about it; and, my life seems much less stressful.

Also, in regard to the fear of closed or crowded areas (especially elevators); so far, I have only tested the results on a small elevator with four people (it was, however, crowded). In this case, I felt none of my usual anxiety or suffocating feeling I usually feel in such cases."

Linda Hall
Long Beach, CA

Fear of Speaking in Front of Large Groups

"I have had a fear of speaking in front of groups for as long as I can remember. Recently I found that, my inability to speak at work was costing me a good amount of money. Even though I knew all the people in the audience and had no problem talking with them individually or in informal small groups, I still could not address them as a whole. I would usually hire someone to address them, which usually was not effective. Anyway, using Dr. Callahan's technique on myself, I was able to overcome my fears in one day. I actually enjoy public speaking now."

William Perry
Westlake, CA

Fear of Public Speaking

"Before your five minute treatment I was terrified at the prospect of speaking before the most prominent executives at the company where I was employed. After the treatment, I was able to address thirty of our senior management executives without experiencing any fear of feelings of anxiety. As a result, I was able to think and speak with usual clarity.

I was so impressed with the results of the treatment, I decided to use it on my own employees with tremendous results. Some of the problems I have successfully treated include fear of talking on the telephone, fear of conflict in dealing with difficult co-workers, fear of inadequacy, on-the-job emotional outbursts, and even a traumatic childhood fear of dogs.

I have successfully incorporated your treatment into my day-to-day work activities and consider it an accepted and productive part of my management style."

Vaughn E. Kraft
Anaheim, CA

General Fear and Anxiety

"I am an actress, and like many of my colleagues, I have experienced a great deal of fear, anxiety and stress associated with my work. They have been a problem for some time and although they didn't get in the way of my work, they have sometimes prevented me from being able to achieve all that I know I am capable of in my profession.

After experiencing Dr. Callahan's "Five Minute" cure the fears went completely away, painlessly and immediately. I am much freer, have more creativity and experience more pleasure from my work. I feel that I have much more control over my ultimate success."

Rina Lee Bennett
Hollywood, CA

(Appears regularly on CBS, ABC and NBC television, including such shows as: Cagney and Lacey, Archie Bunker's Place, All in the Family, General Hospital, The Young and the Restless, HBO Comedy Playhouse and feature films as well as numerous commercials.)

Fear of Spiders

"I have had a severe fear of spiders since I was a child. If I was cornered by a spider in a shower I would go in the corner and scream for help. I would be unable to get out as long as the spider was there. I was unable to kill any spider because I just was too afraid to get close enough. If I saw a spider even on TV or movies I would be petrified. If a spider ever crawled on me I would go into a totally helpless panic until rescued. I would feel the terrible effects for hours later. Even toy spiders would give me the chills.

It took Dr. Callahan about two and a half minutes to cure this life-long fear. After the treatment I was able to play with some toy spiders with complete comfort.

The next day I was confronted with a spider on the kitchen counter and I was able to walk right over to it with a paper towel and kill it without a second thought; something I was never able to do before and I am now thirty-five years old.

I'm not even conscious of spiders anymore."

Deborah George
Southfield, MI

Fear of Heights

"Without having the vaguest idea of how it works, or why, I can only report that after five minutes with Roger and his phobia cure my previous, lifelong fear of heights simply vanished. The afternoon after Roger worked with me, as a matter of fact, I was standing on a friend's fourth floor balcony — on the outside of the railing?"

Karl Hess
Kearneysville, W.VA

Fear of Heights

"I have a fear of heights when looking out of a window of approximately five stories and up.

The feeling consisted of losing control of my balance, falling foward, dizziness, and also of somehow being sucked (as if a vacuum was pulling me) out of the window — a complete loss of control.

After being treated by Dr. Callahan, I can now look out a window with the feeling of being on ground level."

Diane DeRosa
Los Angeles, CA

Fear of Eating

"A friend of mine's child — he was less than three years old at the time — developed a fear of eating. He had choked on some food and was afraid to eat anything solid. He was taken to their family doctor who told them just to wait it out. The child's fears continued to increase. Dr. Callahan was informed and treated the child's phobia. The child was instructed in Dr. Callahan's techniques and told to use them when he felt fearful (he wasn't confident that the fear would not return). The child used this technique for a few days and quietly forgot about his fears. He is now six years old."

William Perry
Westlake, CA

Statements From Professionals

"Having witnessed you demonstrate your phobia treatment technique on a number of occasions, and having utilized it with my own therapy clients, I must tell you that I am overwhelmingly impressed by its speed and effectiveness — far surpassing any other phobia treatment of which I have knowledge. I think your innovation in this field will stand as an enormous contribution."

Nathaniel Branden, Ph.D.
Author of: **The Psychology of Self Esteem,**
The Disowned Self,
Honoring The Self, and
The Psychology of Romantic Love
Beverly Hills, CA

"I have found the techniques of kinesiology that you have developed fascinating and innovative. These techniques for the treatment of phobias will undoubtedly require psychologists to re-examine our theoretical understanding of the causes and treatment of such problems. If the empirical studies validate the success of your treatment of phobias. I feel your techniques will become one of the most significant landmarks in the treatment of phobias."

Lawrence Onoda Ph.D.
Director of Clinical Psychology
Victory-Tampa Psychological Center
Reseda, CA

"Following our training session several weeks ago, I had occasion to work with a 45 year old business woman who had been suffering from severe claustrophobia for over four years. Her husband had told me that she was in a frantic state because she was unable to ride elevators and was terrified to the point of hysteria whenever she was enclosed in a small space. Their personal and professional lives were being severly restricted.

I spent a half hour with her, five minutes of which I used the techniques you taught me. As we walked out of our session, she greeted her husband with a huge smile and said "Let's go to the office building next door. I want to show you something." We went to the twelve story office building next door, got in an elevator and rode up to the top, got off, walked around and then rode another elevator down to the lobby. During this adventure, her husband kept staring at her in disbelief, and kept asking her if she were all right. She assured both of us that she was completely comfortable. They have since taken a business trip during which she experienced no discomfort (she had been avoiding travel).

I have been using the techniques with many other clients with similar results. I am convinced that this is the most powerful phobia therapy of all time. It is amazing to me that such a simple, efficient process can produce such lasting results in only minutes. I believe you are onto something spectacular!

You have always been on the cutting edge of new and valuable approaches to therapy. It is one of the many things I admire and respect about you. Keep up the good work!"

Lee M. Shulman, Ph.D.
Beverly Hills, CA

"Dr. Roger Callahan has progressed in the last several years which I have known him from an extremely gifted psychotherapist to an innovator whose work and potential help will now be able to reach tens of thousands through *Five Minute Phobia Cure.*

Over the past few years I have been happy to refer many of my patients who have had phobias and have been gratified repeatedly by the results Dr. Callahan produced in a very short time.

The *Five Minute Phobia Cure* is clearly written and demonstrates to the reader step by step the simplicity of the treatment. Considering the low cure rate, the time and expense involved in all of the currently accepted therapies for phobias, Dr. Callahan's discoveries are unique and spectacular.

In medical school, one of the lessons stressed is that harm should not come to the patient by the treatment given. Dr. Callahan's treatment follows those teachings more closely than many medical treatments now in vogue. Even so, this approach will be difficult for many to accept, because kinesiology is so foreign to anything known in Western cultures as therapeutic.

Those with an open mind and a willingness to accept that knowledge and truth extends far beyond our current and past stores of facts will be enriched by Dr. Callahan's findings presented in the *Five Minute Phobia Cure.*

We have been taught that anything that seems too good to be true probably isn't. Dr. Callahan's Five Minute Phobia Cure is the exception that proves the rule."

Harvey M. Ross, MD
Author of:
Fighting Depression, Hypoglycemia
Los Angeles, CA

"I have found the results of Dr. Callahan's psychological reversal technique to be nothing short of amazing. This is the most powerful procedure for dealing with the emotional side of the health triangle I've come across to date! Patients leave my office feeling euphoric, empowered, and positive. Patients with chronic, unresponsive health problems have started responding normally after the reversal work. Several hiatal hernia and endocrine cases cleared spontaneously after having their reversals corrected!

I feel that this will be an extremely valuable technique for all members of the health-care community."

Dr. James D. Hogg
Chiropractic Specialist in Applied Kinesiology
Rock Island, IL

"Just a quick note to tell you about the success I had with a woman this week who has been suffering from a severe phobic response to dirt and contamination for 35 years, and who has engaged in compulsive hand-washing, washing of clothing, and cleaning of all her surroundings. This has severely limited her in every way, because 10 to 12 hours of every day had to be spent cleaning herself and all that surround her.

I used your treatment on three successive days this week, treating each discrete manifestation of the overall phobia individually. The husband reports that on the second day I saw here, she got into bed between the clean sheets, and ordinarily, once she is in bed, she would not get out for fear of contamination. On this occasion, she jumped out of bed, got some medication she had forgotten, and then got right back into bed without washing again. She did not even realize that she had done it. He was amazed and very pleased."

Joyce Shulman, Ph.D.
Beverly Hills, CA

References

Bandler, R. and Grinder, J., Frogs Into Princess, Moah, Utah. Real People Press, 1979.

Diamond, John, Behavioral Kinesiology. New York, Harper and Row. 1979.

Ellis, Albert, Reason and Emotion in Psychotherapy. New York, Lyle Stuart. 1962.

Goodheart, George, International College of Applied Kinesiology, Research Tapes (Monthly Reports). 1980-84.

Gunn, W.B., Walker, M.K., and Day, H.D., Neuro Linguistic Programming: Method Or Myth? J. Counseling Psychology, 1982, Vol 29, No. 3, 327-330.

Malleson, Nicholas, Panic and Phobia, Lancet, 1959, 1-225.

Pines, Maya, Anxiety Diseases, American Health, pp 72-76, June, 84, 1984.

Pitts, Ferris, The Biochemistry of Anxiety. Scientific American, Vol 220, No 2, Feb., 1969, pp 69-75.

Salter, Andrew, Conditioned Reflex Therapy, Creative Age Press, New York, 1949/

Saunders, Geraldine and Ross, Harvey, Hypoglycemia. Pinnacle Books, New York, 1980.

Walther, David, Applied Kinesiology. Vol I, 1981, Systems DC, 275 West Abriendo Ave., Pueblo, Colorado, 81004.

Wolpe, Joseph, Our Useless Fears. Houghton-Mifflin, Boston, 1981.

Note: In Chapter 1 Drs. DuPont and Klein are quoted from the above article by Pines.

Index